ESSAYS AND ADDRESSES
IN WAR TIME

ESSAYS AND ADDRESSES
IN WAR TIME

Bryce, James Bryce, Viscount, 1838-1922,

BY
THE RIGHT HON. VISCOUNT BRYCE
O. M.
(JAMES BRYCE)

Essay Index Reprint Series

BOOKS FOR LIBRARIES PRESS
FREEPORT, NEW YORK

First Published 1918
Reprinted 1968

LIBRARY OF CONGRESS CATALOGUE CARD NUMBER:

68-16914

PRINTED IN THE UNITED STATES OF AMERICA

PREFACE

THIS book contains three essays, written in the first two years of the war to explain to neutral nations the aims, and justify the action, of Great Britain. They are followed by three Addresses of a non-political character, treating of war in general, its causes and some of its phenomena, its social effects, its relation to human progress. The last two essays now appear in print for the first time. They have been written very recently, with a view to that close of the war which seems to be rapidly approaching. One of them examines the history and the meaning of what is called the principle of Nationality, and sets forth briefly the questions requiring the application of that principle which will arise when a treaty of peace has to be made, and the demands of peoples, or parts of peoples, dissatisfied with their present rulers, have to be met. The eighth and last chapter deals with the idea or plan of a League of Nations to enforce peace — a subject on which the author has had the advantage since the first months of the war of a constant correspondence with American friends. It is intended not so much to advocate the formation of such a League — for that seems now to be finding general acceptance — as to set out briefly what the functions of such a League might be, what organs it would need for the discharge of those functions, what objections have been taken to it, what are the answers to such objections, and what are the conditions of our time which may encourage hopes for its success.

There is, in the first three essays, some amount of

repetition, which may, it is hoped, be to some extent excused on the ground that as these essays present what is practically the same subject from different points of view, it was sometimes necessary to state the same facts in different relations. The facts themselves are so strange and yet in the swift passage of events so apt to be imperfectly remembered, that they deserve to be re-stated.

The whole volume was in print before the startling events of October had brought the close of the war so much nearer. The earlier essays are left unchanged, because they were written to convey to foreign readers a concise and so far as possible unbiassed account of the motives and temper, the views and moral judgments with which Britain was prosecuting the war at a time when its issue, though certain to ourselves, appeared doubtful to many foreign observers. It seems better to leave them to speak from the days when Englishmen were bewildered by the doctrines as well as the conduct of their enemies, and were seeking explanations of what was so new to their experience. The clouds are now beginning to lift, already we understand some things better than we did three or four years ago, and we hope to learn much more. Happily that which we most desired has come to pass. This is a war of principles, and the course of events has vindicated the principles of morality and humanity that were at stake.

October 12, 1918.

CONTENTS

CHAPTER I

NEUTRAL NATIONS AND THE WAR

Prefatory Note, written in October 1918

THIS article, written and published in the autumn of 1914, is now reprinted in its original form, in order that it may show what was the impression produced upon Englishmen by the events of the first two months of war. The audacious avowal by the German Government of the doctrine that military necessity warrants breaches of international good faith and common right, and the declarations which were then first brought to the notice of the British people, proceeding from eminent German authorities, that the State stands above all morality and all human feeling, and may adopt any war methods conducive to success, were accompanied by an unprovoked invasion of Belgium and by the savage treatment of its non-combatant inhabitants. That invasion and the attempts to justify it struck us with an amazement it is well to recall, for now, after four years of war, no action, however outrageous, on the part of the enemy Powers surprises us. It seems proper, therefore, to let what was written in 1914 stand unchanged as some evidence of what we then felt, and of our unwillingness to believe that the pernicious theory proclaimed by German writers, and the practice which went almost beyond the theory, could be approved by the German people, whom some of us had known in earlier years as a humane and kindly

I

people, a people whose literature we had admired, and for whose services to learning and science we were grateful.

But if these pages were to be now rewritten, I should be bound to write them differently, and should have to recognize that the view such Englishmen then took was more indulgent than it could have been if we had known and understood the change which had passed upon the German mind since 1870. It is difficult now to cling to the hope expressed in 1914 that the principles avowed by the German Government and put in practice by its High Command were held by only a small minority of the nation.

Allowance must doubtless be made in judging the attitude of the German people, not only for the excitement evoked by a tremendous crisis, which made any criticism of their rulers seem unpatriotic and for the fear of Russia which then possessed them, but also for the mendacity with which the Government, through its pliant tool the German press, have tricked and misled their credulous and submissive subjects. Public opinion is, and has long been, manufactured by the Government, partly through the newspapers, partly owing to the deference paid to declarations proceeding from it. A friend who lived in Germany till 1913, and knows it thoroughly, writes to me: " German opinion is very ill-educated and very ill-informed politically. The pressure on public and private opinion is enormous; a German needs to be a superman if he would stand out boldly for his convictions; and supermen, if they exist, are rare."

Ever since the war began the people have been fed up with falsehoods. The aims and motives of Britain and the United States have been persistently misrepresented. Baseless calumnies have been propagated re-

garding the conduct of British soldiers and sailors,
while the offences committed on sea and land, by order
of the German High Command, have been either concealed or covered up by a tissue of deceits. Concealed,
also, were the massacres of the Eastern Christians perpetrated by those " trusty Turkish Allies," whom the
German Government took to its bosom, and when
German missionaries sought to publish the facts they
were promptly silenced. A strict and stern censorship
has repressed every attempt to make the truth known,
has forbidden criticism, and stifled the voice of truth.
Deeds at which the world grew pale are perhaps hardly
more known to the German peasant or artizan than
to the black soldiers of Germany in Africa.

Yet, after every allowance has been made, it remains
a marvel that in a nation like Germany so few of the
leaders, in learning, science, education, and, above all,
in religion, should have been found bold enough to
condemn, and so many ready to defend, crimes which
some at least among them must have known, and which
would have shocked the generations of Kant and
Goethe and Schiller, of Savigny and Schleiermacher
and Neander. What has become of the nation's conscience?

The explanation some have that the university
teachers and the clergy of the Churches recognized by
the State are in bondage to the Government does not
suffice. There must have been some other cause at
work to produce this callousness. Patriotism itself
must have been perverted by false teachings and bad
examples. I have tried in two later chapters (Essay
III. and Essay VI.) to indicate some of the influences
which may have engendered this extravagant nationalism and sown the seeds of this moral decline which
make the new Germany unlike the old.

The present war has had some unexpected consequences. It has called the attention of the world outside Germany to certain amazing doctrines proclaimed
there, which strike at the root of all international
morality, as well as of all international law, and which
threaten a return to the primitive savagery when every
tribe was wont to plunder and massacre its neighbours.

These doctrines may be found set forth in the widely
circulated book of General von Bernhardi, entitled
Germany and the Next War, published in 1911, and
professing to be mainly based on the teachings of the
famous professor of history, Heinrich von Treitschke.

To readers in other countries, and, I trust, to most
readers in Germany also, these doctrines will appear to
be an outburst of militarism run mad, the product
of a brain intoxicated by the love of war and by super-
heated national self-consciousness.

They would have deserved little notice, much less
refutation, but for one deplorable fact, viz. that action
has recently been taken by the Government of a great
nation (though, as we venture to hope, without the
approval of that nation) which is consonant with them,
and seems to imply a belief in their soundness.

This fact is the conduct of the German Imperial
Government, in violating the neutrality of Belgium,
which Prussia, as well as Great Britain and France,
had solemnly guaranteed by a treaty (made in 1839
and renewed in 1870) ; in invading Belgium when she
refused to allow her armies to pass through to attack
France, although France, the other belligerent, had
solemnly undertaken not to enter Belgium; and in
treating the Belgian cities and people, against whom she
had no cause of quarrel, with a harshness unprecedented
in the history of modern European warfare.

What are these doctrines? I do not for a moment

attribute them to the learned class in Germany, for whom I have profound respect, recognizing their immense services to science and learning; nor to the bulk of the civil administration, a body whose capacity and uprightness are known to all the world; and least of all to the German people generally. That the latter hold no such views appears from General Bernhardi's own words, for he repeatedly complains of, and deplores the pacific tendencies of, his fellow-countrymen.[1]

Nevertheless, the fact that the action referred to, which these doctrines seem to have prompted, and which cannot be defended except by them, has been actually taken, and has thus brought into this war Great Britain, whose interests and feelings made her desire peace, renders it proper to call attention to them and to all that they involve.

I have certainly no prejudice in the matter, for I have been one of those who for many years laboured to promote good relations between Germans and Englishmen, peoples that ought to be friends, and that never before had been enemies, and I had hoped and believed till the beginning of August 1914 that there would be no war, because Belgian neutrality would be respected.

Nor was it only for the sake of Britain and Germany that the English friends of peace sought to maintain good feeling. We had hoped, as some leading German statesmen had hoped, that a friendliness with Germany might enable Britain, with the co-operation of the United States (our closest friends), to mitigate the long antagonism of Germany and of France, with whom we were already on good terms, and to so improve their relations as to secure the general peace of Europe.

---

1 See pp. 10-14 of English translation, and note the phrase, "Aspirations for peace seem to poison the soul of the German people."

Into the causes which frustrated these efforts and so suddenly brought on this war I will not enter. Many others have dealt with them.[1] Moreover, the facts, at least as we in England see and believe them, and as the documents seem to prove them to be, appear not to be known to the German people, and the motives of the chief actors have not yet been fully ascertained.

One thing, however, I can confidently declare. It was neither commercial rivalry nor jealousy of German power that brought Britain into the field. Nor was there any hatred in the British people for Germany, nor any wish to break German power. Even now, we have no enmity to the German people. The leading political thinkers and historians of England had given hearty sympathy to the efforts made by the German people (from 1815 to 1866 and 1870) to attain political unity, as they had sympathized with the parallel efforts of the Italians.

The two peoples, German and British, were of kindred race, and linked by many ties. In both countries there were doubtless some persons who desired war, and whose writings, apparently designed to provoke it, did much to misrepresent the general national sentiment. But these persons were, as I believe, a small minority in both countries.

So far as Britain was concerned, it was the invasion of Belgium that arrested all efforts to avert war, and made even the best friends of peace join in holding that the duty of fulfilling their treaty obligations to a weak State was paramount to every other consideration.

I return to the doctrines set forth by General von

---

[1] [A clear and strong light has recently been thrown upon the circumstances preceding the outbreak of the war by the recently published memorandum of Prince Lichnowsky, who was then German Ambassador in London. They fully vindicate the motives and action in those critical days of Sir Edward Grey, who was then Foreign Secretary.— *Oct.* 1918.]

Bernhardi, and apparently accepted by the military caste to which he belongs. Briefly summed up, they are as follows. His own words are used, except when it becomes necessary to abridge a lengthened argument:

War is in itself a good thing. " It is a biological necessity of the first importance " (p. 18).

" The inevitableness, the idealism, the blessings of war, as an indispensable and stimulating law of development must be repeatedly emphasized " (p. 37).

" War is the greatest factor in the furtherance of culture and power."

" Efforts to secure peace are extraordinarily detrimental as soon as they influence politics " (p. 28).

" Fortunately these efforts can never attain their ultimate objects in a world bristling with arms, where a healthy egotism still directs the policy of most countries. ' God will see to it,' says Treitschke, ' that war always recurs as a drastic medicine for the human race ' " (p. 36).

" Efforts directed towards the abolition of war are not only foolish, but absolutely immoral, and must be stigmatized as unworthy of the human race " (p. 34).

Courts of arbitration are pernicious delusions. " The whole idea represents a presumptuous encroachment on the natural laws of development which can only lead to the most disastrous consequences for humanity generally " (p. 34).

" The maintenance of peace never can be or may be the goal of a policy " (p. 25).

" Efforts for peace would, if they attained their goal, lead to general degeneration, as happens everywhere in Nature, where the struggle for existence is eliminated " (p. 35).

Huge armaments are in themselves desirable. "They are the most necessary precondition of our national health" (p. 11).

"The end all and be all of a State is Power, and he who is not man enough to look this truth in the face should not meddle with politics" (quoted from Treitschke *Politik*) (p. 45).

"The State's highest moral duty is to increase its power" (pp. 45-6).

"The State is justified in making conquests whenever its own advantage seems to require additional territory" (p. 46).

"Self-preservation is the State's highest ideal," and justifies whatever action it may take, if that action be conducive to the end.

The State is the sole judge of the morality of its own action. It is, in fact, above morality, or, in other words, Whatever is necessary is moral.

"Recognized rights (*i.e.* treaty rights) are never absolute rights; they are of human origin, and therefore imperfect and variable. There are conditions in which they do not correspond to the actual truth of things; in this case the infringement of the right appears morally justified" (p. 49). In fact, the State is a law to itself.

"Every sovereign State has the undoubted right to declare war at its pleasure, and is consequently entitled to repudiate its treaties" (Treitschke).

"Weak nations have not the same right to live as the powerful and vigorous nation" (p. 34).

"Any action in favour of collective humanity outside the limits of the State and nationality is impossible" (p. 25).

These are startling propositions, though propounded as practically axiomatic. They are not new, for twenty-two centuries ago the sophist Thrasymachus in Plato's *Republic* argued (Socrates refuting him) that Justice is nothing more than the advantage of the Stronger, *i.e.* Might is Right.[1]

The most startling among them is the denial that there are any duties owed by the State to Humanity, except that of imposing its own superior civilization upon as large a part of humanity as possible, and the denial of the duty of observing treaties. Treaties are only so much paper.[2]

To modern German writers the State is a much more tremendous entity than it is to Englishmen or Americans. It is a supreme power with a sort of mystic sanctity, a power conceived of, as it were, self-created, a force altogether distinct from, and superior to, the persons who compose it.

But a State is, after all, only so many individuals organized under a Government. It is no wiser, no more righteous than the human beings of whom it consists, and whom it sets up to govern it.

Has the State, then, no morality, no responsibility?

If it is right for persons united as citizens into a State to rob and murder for their collective advantage by their collective power, why should it be wicked for the citizens as individuals to do so? Does their moral responsibility cease when and because they act together? Most legal systems hold that there are acts which one man may lawfully do which become unlawful if done by a number of men conspiring together. But now it would seem that what would be a crime in persons as

---

1 Plato lays down that the end for which a State exists is Justice.

2 There are, of course, cases in which a treaty may become obsolete by a complete change in the conditions under which it was made, as the treaties of Vienna of 1815 had become obsolete sixty years afterwards. But the case of Belgium was not such a case, nor can so-called "military necessity" ever justify violation. The Hague Convention of 1907 expressly provides that belligerents must respect neutral territory.

individuals is high policy for those persons united in a State.[1]

Is there no such thing as a common humanity? Are there no duties owed to it? Is there none of that " decent respect to the opinion of mankind " which the framers of the Declaration of Independence recognized; no sense that even the greatest States are amenable to the sentiment of the civilized world?

Let us see how these doctrines affect the smaller and weaker States which have hitherto lived in comparative security beside the Great Powers.

They will be absolutely at the mercy of the stronger. Even if protected by treaties guaranteeing their neutrality and independence they will not be safe, for treaty obligations are worthless " when they do not correspond to facts," *i.e.* when the strong Power finds that they stand in its way. Its interests are paramount.

If a State has valuable minerals, as Sweden has iron, and Belgium coal, and Rumania oil, or if it has abundance of water-power, like Norway, Sweden, and Switzerland, or if it holds the mouth of a navigable river the upper course of which belongs to another nation, the great State may conquer and annex that small State as soon as it finds that it needs the minerals, or the water-power, or the river mouth.

It has the Power, and Power gives Right. The interests, the sentiments, the patriotism and love of independence of the small people go for nothing.

Civilization has turned back upon itself, culture is to expand its domain by barbaric force. Governments derive their authority, not from the consent of the

1 General Bernhardi (following Treitschke) refers approvingly to Machiavelli as " the first who declared that the keynote of every policy was the advancement of power." The Florentine, however, was not the preacher of doctrines with which he sought, like the General, to edify his contemporaries. He merely took his Italian world as he saw it. He did not attempt to buttress his maxims by false philosophy, false history, and false science.

governed, but from the weapons of the conqueror.
Law and morality between nations have vanished.
Herodotus tells us that the Scythians worshipped as
their God a naked sword. That is the deity to be
installed in the place once held by the God of Christianity, the God of righteousness and mercy.

States, mostly despotic States, have sometimes applied parts of this system of doctrine, but none has proclaimed it. The Romans, conquerors of the world,
were not a scrupulous people, but even they stopped
short of these principles. Certainly they never set
them up as an ideal. Neither did those magnificent
Saxon and Swabian Emperors of the Middle Ages
whose fame General von Bernhardi is fond of recall-
ing. They did not enter Italy as conquerors, claiming
her by the right of the strongest. They came on the
faith of a legal title, which, however fantastic it may
seem to us to-day, the Italians themselves — and, indeed, the whole of Latin Christendom — admitted.
Dante, the greatest and most patriotic of Italians, welcomed the Germanic Emperor Henry the Seventh into
Italy, and wrote a famous book to prove his claims,
vindicating them on the ground that he, as the heir of
Rome, stood for Law and Right and Peace. The
noblest title which those Emperors chose to bear was
that of *Imperator Pacificus,* bestowed upon the first
of them when he was crowned in Rome in A.D. 800. In
the Middle Ages, when men were always fighting, they
appreciated the blessings of war much less than does
General Bernhardi, and they valued peace, not war, as
a means to civilization and culture. They had not
learnt in the school of Treitschke that peace means
decadence and war is the true civilizing influence.

The doctrines above stated are (as I have tried to
point out) well calculated to alarm the small States

which prize their liberty and their individuality, and have been thriving under the safeguard of treaties. But there are also other considerations affecting those States which ought to appeal to men in all countries, to strong nations as well as weak nations.

The small States, whose absorption is now threatened, have been potent and useful — perhaps the most potent and useful — factors in the advance of civilization. It is in them and by them that most of what is most precious in religion, in philosophy, in literature, in science, and in art has been produced.

The first great thoughts that brought man into a true relation with God came from a tiny people, inhabiting a country smaller than Denmark. The religions of mighty Babylon and populous Egypt have vanished: the religion of Israel remains in its earlier as well as in that later form which has overspread the world.

The Greeks were a small people, not united in one great State, but scattered over coasts and among hills in petty city communities, each with its own life, slender in numbers, but eager, versatile, intense. They gave us the richest, the most varied, and the most stimulating of all literatures.

When poetry and art reappeared, after the long night of the Dark Ages, their most splendid blossoms flowered in the small republics of Italy.

In modern Europe what do we not owe to little Switzerland, lighting the torch of freedom 600 years ago, and keeping it alight through all the long centuries when despotic monarchies held the rest of the European Continent; and what to free Holland, with her great men of learning and her painters surpassing those of all other countries save Italy?

So the small Scandinavian nations have given to the world-famous men of science, from Linnaeus down-

wards, poets like Tegnér and Björnson, scholars like
Madvig, dauntless explorers like Fridtjof Nansen.
England had, in the age of Shakespeare, Bacon, and
Milton, a population little larger than that of Bulgaria
to-day. The United States, in the days of Washing-
ton and Franklin and Jefferson and Hamilton and
Marshall, counted fewer inhabitants than Denmark or
Greece.

In the two most brilliant generations of German
literature and thought, the age of Kant and Lessing
and Goethe, of Hegel and Beethoven and Schiller and
Fichte, there was no real German State at all, but a
congeries of principalities and free cities, independent
centres of intellectual life, in which letters and science
produced a richer crop than the two succeeding generations have raised, just as Britain, also, with eight times
the population of the year 1600, has had no more
Shakespeares or Miltons.

No notion is more palpably contradicted by history
than that relied on by the school to which General
Bernhardi belongs, that " culture "— literary, scientific,
and artistic — flourishes best in great military States.
The decay of art and literature in the Roman World
began just when Rome's military power had made that
world one great and ordered State. The opposite view
would be much nearer the truth; though one must admit that no general theory regarding the relations of
art and letters to Governments and political conditions
has ever yet been proved to be sound.[1]

The world is already too uniform, and is becoming
more uniform every day. A few leading languages, a

---

1 General Bernhardi's knowledge of current history may be estimated by the
fact that he assumes (1) that trade rivalry makes a war probable between
Great Britain and the United States! (2) that he believes the Indian princes
and peoples likely to revolt against Britain should she be involved in war!! and
(3) that he expects her self-governing Colonies to take such an opportunity of
severing their connection with her!!!

few forms of civilization, a few types of character, are spreading out from the seven or eight greatest States and extinguishing the weaker languages, forms, and types.

Although the great States are stronger and more populous, their peoples are not necessarily more gifted, and the extinction of the minor languages and types would be a misfortune for the world's future development.

We may not be able to arrest the forces which seem to be making for that extinction, but we certainly ought not to strengthen them. Rather we ought to maintain and defend the smaller States, and to favour the rise and growth of new peoples. Not merely because they were delivered from tyranny of Sultans like Abdul Hamid did the intellect of Europe welcome the successively won liberations of Greece, Servia, Bulgaria, and Montenegro; it was also in the hope that those countries would in time develop out of their present relatively crude conditions new types of culture, new centres of productive intellectual life.

General Bernhardi invokes History, the ultimate court of appeal. He appeals to Caesar. To Caesar let him go. As Schiller wrote: *Die Weltgeschichte ist das Weltgericht.*[1]

History declares that no nation, however great, is entitled to try to impose its type of civilization on others. No race, not even the Teutonic or the Anglo-Saxon, is entitled to claim the leadership of humanity. Each people has in its time contributed something that was distinctively its own, and the world is far richer thereby than if any one race, however gifted, had established a permanent ascendancy.

We of the English-speaking race do not claim for

[1] World History is the World-tribunal.

ourselves, any more than we admit in others, any right
to dominate by force or to impose our own type of
civilization on less powerful races.   Perhaps we have
not that assured conviction of its superiority which the
school of General Bernhardi expresses for the Teutons
of North Germany.   We know how much we owe,
even within our own islands, to the Celtic race.   And
though we must admit that peoples of Anglo-Saxon
stock have, like others, made some mistakes and sometimes abused their strength, let it be remembered what
have been the latest acts they have done abroad.

The United States have twice withdrawn their troops
from Cuba, which they could easily have retained.
They have resisted all temptations to annex any part of
the territories of Mexico, in which the lives and property of their citizens were for three years in constant
danger.   So Britain also restored in 1906-7 the am-
plest self-government to the two South African Republics, which had been in arms against her thirteen
years ago (having already agreed to the maintenance
on equal terms of the Dutch language), and the citizens
of those Republics have now spontaneously come forward to support her by arms, under the gallant leader
who then commanded the Boer forces.   Nor should
we forget that one reason why the princes of India
have rallied so promptly and heartily to Britain in this
war is because for many years past we have avoided
annexing the territories of those princes, allowing them
to adopt heirs when successors of their own families
failed, and leaving to them as much as possible of the
ordinary functions of government.

It is only vulgar minds that mistake bigness for
greatness, for greatness is of the Soul, not of the Body.
In the judgment which history will hereafter pass upon
the forty centuries of recorded progress towards civili-

zation that now lie behind us, what are the tests it will apply to determine the true greatness of a people?

Not population, not territory, not wealth, not military power. Rather will history ask: What examples of lofty character and unselfish devotion to honour and duty has a people given? What has it done to increase the volume of knowledge? What thoughts and what ideals of permanent value and unexhausted fertility has it bequeathed to mankind? What works has it produced in poetry, music, and the other arts to be an unfailing source of enjoyment to posterity?

The smaller peoples need not fear the application of such tests.

The world advances not, as the Bernhardi school suppose, only or even mainly by fighting. It advances mainly by Thinking and by a process of reciprocal teaching and learning, by a continuous and unconscious cooperation of all its strongest and finest minds.

Each race — Hellenic and Italic, Celtic and Teutonic, Iberian and Slavonic — has something to give, each something to learn; and when their blood is blent the mixed stock may combine the gifts of both.

The most progressive races have been those who combined willingness to learn with a strength which enabled them to receive without loss to their own quality, retaining their primal vigour, but entering into the labours of others, as the Teutons who settled within the dominions of Rome profited by the lessons and examples of the old civilization.

Let me disclaim once more before I close any intention to attribute to the German people the principles set forth by the school of Treitschke and Bernhardi, their hatred of peace and arbitration, their disregard of treaty obligations, their scorn for the weaker peoples.

We in England would feel an even deeper sadness

than weighs upon us now if we could suppose that such principles had been embraced by a nation whose thinkers have done so much for human progress and who have produced so many shining examples of Christian saintliness.

But when those principles have been ostentatiously proclaimed, when a peaceful neutral country which the other belligerent had undertaken to respect has been invaded and treated as Belgium has been treated, and when attempts are made to justify these deeds as incidental to a campaign for civilization and culture, it becomes necessary to point out how untrue and how pernicious such principles are.

What are the teachings of history, history to which General Bernhardi is fond of appealing? That war has been the constant handmaid of tyranny and the source of more than half the miseries of man. That although some wars have been necessary, and have given occasion for the display of splendid heroism — wars of defence against aggression, or to succour the oppressed — most wars have been needless or unjust. That the mark of an advancing civilization has been the substitution of friendship for hatred and of peaceful for warlike ideals. That small peoples have done and can do as much for the common good of humanity as large peoples. That treaties must be observed, for what are they but records of national faith solemnly pledged, and what could bring mankind more surely and swiftly back to that reign of violence and terror from which it has been slowly rising for the last ten centuries than a destruction of trust in the plighted faith of nations?

No event has brought out that essential unity which now exists in the world so forcibly as this war has done, for no event has ever so affected every part of the

world.   Four continents are involved — the whole of
the Old World — and the New World suffers griev-
ously in its trade, industry, and finance.   Thus the
whole world is interested in preventing the recurrence
of such a calamity; and there is a general feeling
throughout the world that an effort must be made to
remove the causes which have brought it upon us.

We are told that armaments must be reduced, that
the baleful spirit of militarism must be quenched, that
the peoples must everywhere be admitted to a fuller
share in the control of foreign policy, that efforts must
be made to establish a sort of League of Concord —
some system of international relations and reciprocal
peace alliances by which the weaker nations may be
protected, and under which differences between nations
may be adjusted by courts of arbitration and conciliation of wider scope than those that now exist.

All these things are desirable.   All nations, and,
most of all, the weaker nations, ought to desire them.
But no scheme for preventing future wars will have any
chance of success unless it rests upon the assurance
that the States which enter into it will loyally and stead-
fastly abide by it, and that each and all of them will
join in coercing by their overwhelming united strength
any State which may disregard the obligations it has
undertaken.

The faith of treaties is the only solid foundation on
which a Temple of Peace can be built up.

CHAPTER II

THE ATTITUDE OF GREAT BRITAIN IN THE PRESENT WAR

WE in Britain who respect and value the opinion of the free neutral peoples of Europe and America cannot but desire that those peoples should be duly informed of the way in which we regard the circumstances and the possible results of the present conflict. The pages which follow have been written in compliance with a request from one of those free countries, Switzerland, but what has been set down to be read by its people may equally well be addressed to other neutrals. I speak here with no more authority than is possessed by any private citizen of my country who has had a long experience of public affairs, and my only wish is to express what I believe to be its general sentiments. Other writers would doubtless convey those sentiments in somewhat different language, but I think they would do so to much the same general effect, for the British Nation is at this crisis united in its views and purposes to an extent almost unprecedented in its history.

I shall not enter into the circumstances which brought about the war, for these have been often stated officially and can be readily understood from documents already published. The evidence contained in those documents ought, it seems to me, to be quite convincing to any impartial mind.[1] All that need be said here is that the

1 It was convincing from the first. But if any further proof be needed the spring of 1918 brought an unexpected and most effective confirmation in the form of a secret memorandum written by Prince Lichnowski (German Am-

British nation did most assuredly neither desire nor contemplate war. There was no hostility to Germany except among a very few persons who thought she was already planning to attack us. The notion which has been assiduously propagated by the German Government, that England desired to bring about war because she feared the commercial competition of Germany and hoped to destroy German productive industry and mercantile prosperity, is absolutely untrue and without the slightest foundation. It is indeed an absurd suggestion, for every man of sense knew that German trade had brought more advantage to our trading classes than any damage German competition had been doing to them. England had far more to lose than to gain by war. Germany was her best foreign customer, taking more goods from her than did any other foreign country. It was plain to the meanest understanding that a war would involve England in pecuniary losses which

bassador in London in 1912–14), and published without his knowledge or consent. In it the ex-Ambassador, who had been conducting negotiations between his country and Britain over various questions affecting their relations, bears the clearest and strongest testimony to the friendly spirit in which the British Government met the wishes of Germany. Large concessions, so large that they seem now, with our fuller knowledge of German plans, too generous, were made regarding the assignment of regions in Africa as spheres of German influence, and as respects the Bagdad railway and Mesopotamia as far as El Basra. Sir Edward Grey, he declares, was sincerely anxious for friendship between the countries, and did his utmost, up to the last moments in July and August, 1914, to avert war. This account of Sir Edward's good-will is confirmed by Herr von Jagow, who was then Foreign Secretary in Germany. The Memorandum also explicitly contradicts the notion, propagated in Germany, that commercial jealousy had made British mercantile men disposed to war. "It was precisely in commercial circles," says Lichnowski, "that I found the liveliest disposition to establish good relations [with Germany] and to promote common economic interests."

Another revelation of high significance is contained in the account given by Mr. Morgenthau, lately American Ambassador at Constantinople (see his articles in *The World's Work* for May and June 1918), of the description given to him by Baron von Wangenheim (till his recent death, German Ambassador to Turkey) of the secret meeting at Potsdam on July 5, 1914, at which the German Emperor asked the heads of the Army, of the Navy, and of the great financial establishments of Germany whether they were all prepared for the approaching war. This meeting is referred to in Prince Lichnowski's Memorandum also, and there seems to be no doubt that war was then virtually decided upon.

must far exceed, and had within the first year of war
far exceeded, any pecuniary gain her traders could
possibly have made by the crippling of German trade
for many a year to come.   One of the reasons why
many Englishmen thought that there was no likelihood
of a war between the two countries was because they
believed that both countries knew what frightful losses
to each the war would bring.   Unluckily they did not
know the mind and temper of the class that was ruling
Germany.   Moreover, the fact that Britain had not
prepared herself for a land war shows how little she
expected it.   She had an army very small in comparison
with those of the Continental powers, and no store of
guns or shell comparable to theirs; so, when the war
broke out — Belgium invaded, France threatened with
destruction — she found herself suddenly obliged to
raise a large force by voluntary enlistment at short notice.   Few supposed that the response of the people
would have been so general and so hearty.   The response came because the nation was united as it had
never been united before in support of any war.   That
which united it at the first moment was the invasion of
Belgium; and that which has done most to keep it
united and to stimulate it to exertions hitherto undreamt
of has been popular indignation at the methods by
which the German Government has conducted hostilities by land and by sea.

The German Government has alleged that the British
Fleet had been mobilized with a view to war.   That is
absolutely untrue.   What happened was this.   The
Fleet had been going through its usual summer manœuvres.   Just as these manœuvres were coming to an
end, a threatening war cloud unexpectedly arose out of
a blue sky.   Most naturally, the ships which would in
the usual course have been dispersed to their accus-

tomed peace stations were commanded not to disperse
until further orders were received.   There was in this
no evidence of any purpose to embark in war, for to
keep the Fleet together was in the circumstances the
obvious and only prudent course.

Now let me try to state what are the principles which
animate the British people, making them believe they
have a righteous cause, and inducing them, because they
so believe, to prosecute the war with their utmost
energy.

There is a familiar expression which we use in England to sum up the position and aims of a nation.   It is,
" What does the nation ' stand for '? "   What are the
principles and the interests which prescribe its course?
What are the ends, over and above its own welfare,
which it seeks to promote?   What is the nature of the
mission with which it feels itself charged?   What are
the ideals which it would like to see prevailing throughout the world?

There are five of these principles or aims or ideals
which I will here set forth, because they stand out conspicuously in the present crisis, though they have all
been more or less parts of the settled policy of Britain.

I. The first of these five is Liberty.

England and Switzerland have been the two modern
countries in which Liberty first took tangible form in
equal laws and in the institutions of self-government.
Every lover of poetry remembers the lines in which
Wordsworth joins these lands as the ancient homes of
freedom:

> Two Voices are there, one is of the Sea,
> One of the Mountains, each a mighty Voice.

For a long time it was in these two countries alone that

liberty maintained its life, while elsewhere feudal oligarchies were being superseded by despotic monarchies.
After a time Holland followed, and the three peoples
of the Scandinavian North, kindred to us in blood,
have followed likewise.

In England Liberty appeared from early days in a
recognition of the right of the citizen to be protected
against arbitrary power and to bear his share in the
work of governing his own community.   It is from
Great Britain that other European countries whose political condition had, from the end of the Middle Ages
down to the end of the eighteenth century, been un-
favourable to freedom, drew, in that and the following
century, their examples of a Government which could be
united and efficient and yet popular, strong to defend
itself against attack, and yet respectful of the rights
of its own members.   The British Constitution has
been the model whence most of the countries that have
within recent times adopted constitutional government
have drawn their institutions.   Britain has herself during the last eighty years made her constitution more
and more truly popular.   It is now as democratic as
that of any other European State, and in their dealings
with other countries, the British people have shown a
constant sympathy with freedom.   They showed it
early in the nineteenth century to Spanish constitutional
reformers and to Greek insurgents against Turkish
tyranny.   They showed it to Switzerland when they
foiled (in 1847) the attempt of Metternich to interfere with her independence.   They have shown it in
other ways within recent years.   Britain has given free
Governments to all those of her colonies in which there
is a population of European origin capable of using
them, and this has confirmed the attachment to herself
of those colonies.   In Canada two insurrections broke

out in 1837–38, insignificant, and easily suppressed. But the warning they gave in revealing local discontent with the existing system was not lost. A new system was set up, discontent quickly disappeared, and some of those who had been in arms against the British Crown were before long its loyal supporters, a few of them even among its Ministers. This became the beginning of that policy of Dominion Self-Government which has so powerfully cemented the different parts of what has been well called the Union of British Commonwealths. In 1907–8, only six years after a war with the two Dutch Republics of South Africa, which had ended by a treaty that brought them into the territories of Britain, she restored self-government to the Transvaal and the Orange Free State, and they soon afterwards became members of the new autonomous Confederation called the Union of South Africa, side by side with the old British colonies of the Cape and Natal. The first Prime Minister of that Union was General Louis Botha, who had been Commander-in-Chief of the Boer forces in their war with Britain. What has been the result? When the present war broke out the German Government, which had long been planning to induce the Transvaal and the Orange Free State to break away from Britain, found to their astonishment that the vast majority of the South African Boers stood heartily by her. General Botha took command of the Union armies, and defeated the German forces in the German colony of South-West Africa without any assistance from British troops.

So in German East Africa General Smuts, who had been one of the most efficient leaders of the Boer forces in the South African War of 1899–1901, was placed in command of the army which drove the German native and white troops out of that region into Portuguese territory and relieved the inhabitants from the harshness of German rule. He has now been for some time a trusted and most valuable member of the British War Cabinet. So much for South African loyalty to the Empire. As regards the other self-governing Dominions, which the Germans expected to take the opportunity this war would have afforded of severing their connection with the Mother Country, every one knows with what ardour and promptitude they placed all their resources at the service of the common cause and with what valour their soldiers have fought for it. These are the fruits of those principles of liberty by which British policy has been guided since those great colonies grew up.

The free citizens of neutral nations ought not to forget that the principles of freedom are involved in the present war. More and more as the struggle goes on has the conduct of the German statesmen and soldiers shown that a Government which spurns Right and rests upon Force is of necessity the enemy of every government that rests upon the will of the people, and will try to crush or fetter liberty wherever it has the chance. Both cannot live side by side. This is the meaning of President Wilson's dictum that "the world must be made safe for democracy." Britain, having stood for liberty through many centuries, naturally became its champion in this decisive hour. The United States, the eldest-born child of the liberty which Englishmen had won for themselves before the separation of 1776, has entered the war from like motives, and is waging it as a crusade.

Political liberty, itself founded on a recognition of the worth of the individual man, has in England borne its appropriate fruit in creating a respect for the rights of every human being of whatever race. England led the way in the abolition of negro slavery. More than eighty years ago her Parliament voted sums, enormous for those days, to liberate slaves in the British colonies. The extinction of the slave trade was due to her missionaries, among whom the honoured name of Livingstone stands first, to her philanthropists at home, to the energy of her naval officers on the Atlantic and Indian Oceans. For the last three generations her Government has everywhere sought to secure the rights and promote the welfare of the native races under her control. Her record is not perfect, for there have now and then been errors, or lapses from the normal standard she prescribed for herself. But compare her long record in this respect with the short but scandalous record of oppression which the German administrators have made for themselves in South-West Africa, in East Africa, and in Togoland. These have been the fruits of Liberty as Britain has understood it and practised it, even before her own Government had taken a democratic form: and they have been profitable for the world.

II. Britain stands for the principle of Nationality. She has always given her sympathy to the efforts of a people restless under a foreign dominion to deliver themselves from the stranger and to be ruled by a Government of their own. The efforts of Greece from 1820 till her liberation from the Turks, the efforts of Italy to shake off the hated yoke of Austria and attain national unity under an Italian King found their warmest support in England. English Liberals gave their sympathy to national movements in Hungary and Poland. Mazzini, Garibaldi, Cavour, Kossuth and Deák were heroes to the British people as Kosciuzko had been to an earlier generation. They gave that sympathy also to the German movement for national unity from 1848 to 1870, for in those days that movement was led by German Liberals of lofty aims who did not desire, as the recent rulers of Germany have desired, to make their national strength a menace to the peace and security of their neighbours. In India, England has long ceased to absorb into her dominions the native States, and has been seeking only to guide the rulers of those States into the paths of just and humane administration, while leaving their internal affairs to their own native Governments. It was not possible to extend a representative system resembling those of England herself to the numerous races that compose the Indian population, because those races were not yet fit to work such a system. A firm and impartial hand is indeed needed to keep the peace among them. But the British Government in India regards, and has long regarded, its power as a trust to be used for the benefit of the people, and in recent years efforts have been made to associate the people more and more with the work of the higher branches of administration and legislation. Hindu and Musulman judges sit beside European judges in the highest Courts, while the vast mass of local administration is conducted by native officials and native magistrates. Now (in 1918) a scheme of far-reaching change has been framed, designed to create representative institutions over nearly the whole of British India, and under these the welfare of the country will be more and more in native hands. No tribute or revenue of any kind has for very many years past been drawn by England from India, and, as every one knows, neither has it been levied from any of those colonies which the Home Government controls. The good results of this policy have been seen in the steady increase of the confidence and good-will of the native rulers and aristocracy of India to the British Government, so that when the present war broke out all those rulers at once offered military aid. Large Indian forces gladly came to fight, and fought most gallantly, in Mesopotamia and in Palestine, where they were opposed to a Muslim enemy, as well as beside the British forces in France.

I do not claim that these successes attained by British ideas and methods are due to any innate and peculiar merits of British character. They may be largely ascribed to the fact that the insular position and the political and social conditions of England enabled her, earlier than most other peoples, both to attain constitutional liberty and to learn to love it and trust it. She has had long experience, and has profited by experience. She has had cause to see how much better it is to govern by justice and in a fair and generous spirit than to rely on brute force. Once in her history, 140 years ago, she lost the North American Colonies because, in days when British freedom was less firmly established than it is now, a narrow-minded and obstinate King induced his Government to treat those colonies with unwise harshness. She has never forgotten that lesson, and has more and more come to see that freedom and nationality are a surer basis for contentment and loyalty than is the application of military power. Compare with the happy results that have followed the instances I have mentioned of respect for liberty and national sentiment in the cases of South Africa and India, as well as in the self-governing Dominions, the results in North Sleswig, in Posen, in Alsace-Lorraine, of the opposite policy of force sternly applied by Prussian statesmen and soldiers.

III. Britain stands for the maintenance of treaty obligations and of those rights of the smaller nations

which rest upon such obligations. The circumstances
of the present war, which saw a peaceful neutral country suddenly attacked by a Power that had itself
solemnly guaranteed the neutrality of its territory,
summoned England to stand up for the defence of those
rights and obligations, for she felt that the good faith
of treaties is the only foundation on which peace between nations can rest, and is, especially, the only guarantee for the security of those which do not maintain
large armies. We recognize the value of the smaller
States, knowing what they have done for the progress
of mankind, grateful for the examples set by many of
them of national heroism and of achievements in science, literature, and art. So far from desiring to see
the smaller peoples absorbed into the larger, as German theorists appear to wish, we believe that the world
would profit if there were in it a greater number of
small peoples, each developing its own type of character and its own forms of thought and art.

Both these principles — the observance of treaties
and the rights of the smaller neutral States — were
raised in the sharpest form by the unprovoked invasion
of Belgium only two days after the German Minister
at Brussels had lulled the uneasiness of the Belgian
Government by his pacific assurances. Such conduct
was a threat to every neutral nation. That which befell Belgium might have befallen Switzerland or Holland had Germany decided that it was to her interests
to attack either of them for the sake of securing a
passage for her armies. England was obliged to come
to Belgium's support and fulfil the obligation she had
herself contracted to defend the neutrality of the country unrighteously attacked. When the German armies
suddenly crossed the Belgian frontier, carrying slaughter and destruction in their train, an issue of transcend-

ent importance was raised. Can treaties be violated with impunity? Is a nation which, trusting to the protection of international justice and treaty obligations, has not so armed itself as to be able to repel invasion, obliged helplessly to submit to see its territory overrun and its towns destroyed? If such violence prevails, what sense of security can any small nation enjoy? Will it not be the helpless prey of some stronger Power, whenever that Power finds an interest in pouncing upon it? What becomes of the whole fabric of international law and international justice? Britain, obliged by honour to succour Belgium, thus became the champion of international right and of the security of the smaller nations. There is nothing she more earnestly desires to obtain as a result of this war than that the smaller States should be placed for the future in a position of safety, in which the guarantees for their independence and peace shall be stronger than before, because the sanction of the law of nations will have been made more effective.

IV. Britain stands for the regulation of the methods of warfare in the interests of humanity, and especially for the exemption of non-combatants from the sufferings and horrors which war brings. Here is another issue raised by the present crisis, another conflict of opposing principles. In the ancient world, and among semi-civilized peoples in more recent times, non-combatant civilians as well as the fighting forces had to bear those sufferings. The men were killed, combatants and non-combatants alike, the women and children, if spared, were reduced to slavery. That is what the gang which now rules Turkey went on doing all through 1915 in Asia Minor and Armenia, on a far larger scale than even the massacres perpetrated by Abdul Hamid in 1895–96. The snake has shed his

old skin, but he is none the less venomous. This gang
of ruffians slaughtered the men, enslaved some of the
women by selling them in open market or seizing them
for the harem, and drove the rest, with the children,
out into deserts to perish from hunger. The Turkish
Government is, of course, a thoroughly barbarous Government, and what surprises those who know its history
is not the spirit it has again displayed, but the con-
nivance or encouragement of the nominally Christian
Government of Germany. But in civilized Europe
Christian nations have, during the last few centuries,
softened the conduct of war by agreeing to respect the
lives and property of innocent non-combatants, and
thus, although the scale of modern wars has been
greater, less misery has been inflicted on inhabitants of
invaded territories. Their sufferings were less in the
eighteenth century than in the seventeenth, and less in
the nineteenth than in the eighteenth. In the war of
1870–71 the German troops, though addicted to the
plunder of houses and sometimes guilty of excesses,
seem on the whole to have behaved better in France
than an invading force had usually behaved in similar
circumstances. Now, however, in this present war,
the German military and naval commanders have taken
a long step backwards towards barbarism. Innocent
non-combatants have been slaughtered by thousands
in Belgium and in France, and the only excuse offered
(for the facts of the slaughter are practically admitted) is that German troops have sometimes been fired
at by civilians. Now it is true that any civilian who
takes up arms without observing the rules prescribed
for civilian resistance, which custom has established
and the Hague Convention has sanctioned, is liable to
be shot. The rules of war permit that. But it is
contrary to the rules of war, as well as to common

justice and humanity, to kill a civilian who has not himself sought to harm an invading force.

German air-war has been conducted with equal inhumanity. Bombs have during three years been dropped upon undefended towns and quiet country villages in eastern and Central England, on places where there are no troops, no war factories, no stores of ammunition. Very few combatants have suffered, and the women and children killed have been far more numerous than the male non-combatants. No military advantage has been gained by these crimes. They have not even frightened the people generally.

The same retrogression towards barbarism is seen in the German conduct of war at sea. It had long been the rule and practice of civilized nations that when a merchant vessel is destroyed by a ship of war because it is impossible to carry the merchant vessel into the port of the captor, the crew and the passengers of the vessel should be taken off and their lives saved, before the vessel is sunk. Common humanity prescribes this, but the German submarines have been sinking unarmed merchant vessels and drowning their passengers and crews without giving them even the opportunity to surrender.

These facts raise an issue in which the interests of all mankind are involved. The German Government claims the right to kill the innocent because it suits their military interests. We deny this right, as all countries ought to deny it. England is contending in this war for humanity against cruelty, and she appeals to the conscience of all the neutral peoples to give her their moral support in this contention. Peoples that are now neutral may suffer in future, just as those innocent persons I have referred to are suffering now by these acts of unprecedented barbarity.

V. England stands for a Pacific as opposed to a Military type of civilization. Her regular army had always been small in proportion to her population, and very small in comparison with the armies of great Continental nations. Although she recognizes that there are some countries in which universal service may be necessary, and times at which it may be necessary in any country, she has preferred to leave her people free to follow their civil pursuits, and had raised her army by voluntary enlistment. Every stranger who before 1914 came to England from the European Continent was struck by the fact that in the streets of her cities there were hardly any soldiers to be seen. Military and naval officers have never, as in Germany, formed a class by themselves, have never been a political power, or exercised political influence. The Cabinet Ministers placed in charge of these two services have always been civilian statesmen — not Generals or Admirals — until the outbreak of the present war, when, for the first time, under the stress of a new emergency, a professional soldier of long experience was placed at the head of the War Department. England has repeatedly sought at European Conferences to bring about a reduction of war armaments, as well as to secure improved rules mitigating the usages of war; but has found her efforts baffled by the opposition of the German Government. In none of the larger countries, except, indeed, in the United States, are the people so generally and sincerely attached to peace.

It may be asked why, if this is so, does England maintain so large a navy. The question deserves an answer. Her navy is maintained for three reasons. The first is, that as her army has been very small she is obliged to protect herself by a strong home fleet from any risk of invasion. She has never forgotten

the lesson of the Napoleonic wars, when it was the
navy that saved her from the fate which befell so many
European countries at Napoleon's hands. Were she
not to keep up this first line of defence at sea, a huge
army and a huge military expenditure in time of peace
would be inevitable. The second reason is that as
England does not produce nearly enough food to support her population, she must draw supplies from other
countries, and would be in danger of starvation if in
war-time she lost the command of the sea. It is therefore vital to her existence that she should be able to
secure the unimpeded import of articles of food. And
the third reason is that England is responsible for the
defence of the coasts and the commerce of her colonies
and other foreign possessions, such as India. These
do not maintain a naval force sufficient for their defence, and the Mother Country is therefore compelled
to have a fleet sufficient to guarantee their safety and
protect their shipping. No other great State has such
far-reaching liabilities, and, therefore, no other needs
a navy so large as Britain must maintain. In this policy there is no warlike or aggressive spirit, no menace
to other countries. It is a measure purely of defence,
costly and burdensome, but borne because her own
safety and that of her colonies absolutely require it.
Neither has Britain used her naval strength to inflict
harm on any other countries. In time of peace she
has not tried to use it to injure the commerce of her
chief industrial competitors. No step was ever taken
to retard the rapid growth of the mercantile marines
of Germany and Norway, both of which have been
immensely developed in recent years. The free and
equal use of ocean highways has, in time of peace, never
been infringed by her. In time of war she doubtless
exercises those rights of maritime blockade, search, and

capture which her naval strength enables her to exert.
But rights of blockade and capture have always been
exerted by every naval power in war time.   They are
a recognized method of war, and were exerted in the
American Civil War fifty years ago, in the war of
France with China, in the war of Chile with Peru, and
in the more recent war between Japan and Russia.
They are not rights newly claimed by Britain, and they
have been exercised with a constant respect for the
lives of non-combatants.

Much has been said since the war began about
" the freedom of the seas."   What sense that phrase
has, or ought to have, I will not venture to enquire.
No two persons seem to use it in the same sense.   In
the German mouth it seems to mean that no State is to
possess a navy larger than Germany's.   The only rational meaning it can have in war time would seem to
be a rule granting the immunity from capture by war-
ships to vessels carrying merchandise or passengers
only.   It is an arguable question whether on a balance
of considerations the right of capture ought or ought not
to be recognized by international law.   Hitherto it
has been recognized, so the British fleet has put it in
force against German ships, and always with due humanity.   In peace time, Britain, as already observed,
has never interfered with the free use of the sea by the
ships, either armed or unarmed, of any other nation.

So far from using her sea-power to the prejudice of
other countries in peace time, and trying by its aid to
promote her own commercial interests, Britain is the
only great country which has opened her doors freely
to the commerce of every other country.   More than
sixty years ago she adopted, and has ever since consistently practised, the policy of free trade.   She im-
poses upon imports no duties intended to protect her

own agriculture or her own manufactures. She gives
no advantages to her own shipping in her own ports,
she pays no bounties to her own shipping, she allows
even coasting trade between her own ports to be open
on equal terms to the ships of all nations. A Dutch or
Swedish or Norwegian vessel may trade from New-
castle to London as freely as a British vessel. And
this free trade policy has been carried out consistently
in all the British colonial possessions. Neither in India, nor in those British colonies whose tariffs are con-
trolled by the Mother Country, are duties imposed
upon foreign imports, except for the purpose of raising
revenue. Such self-governing Dominions as Canada
and Australia have control of their own tariffs and
impose what duties they please — even against the
Mother Country; but that is a part of the self-government which these Dominions have long enjoyed.

The policy of free trade has been supported, and is
valued, in Britain not only on economic grounds, but
also because it is deemed to promote international
peace. Richard Cobden, the first and most powerful
champion in Parliament of that policy, saw in this
tendency its highest value. It is only of that aspect of
the subject that I speak here, because its domestic aspects raise controversies which I do not presume to
enter. He thought that it would so link the nations
together, helping them to know one another, enriching
them all, and making each interested in the prosperity
of the other, each being both a producer and a con-
sumer, each supplying the other's needs and profiting
by the exchange, that each and all would be reluctant
to break the general peace. He was unquestionably
right in principle, although the commercial interests of
Germany in maintaining her trade with England were
not strong enough to overcome the war policy of the

Junker party which expected to extend trade by conquest. The failure of their attempt will hereafter be a warning.   Cobden's hopes have proved to be too sanguine, because he did not foresee — how could he — the selfishness and rapacity of the Junker party and the military caste.   But this idea, that the more the peoples trade freely with one another, the more they will learn that their true interests are not opposed is sound, and has always had great weight in British commercial policy, which has sought for no exclusive advantages, but was content, in the confidence of its own energy, to leave the field open to all competitors.

As an industrial people the English desire peace. They have not worshipped the State, and expected it to conquer markets for them or extort concessions.   They have never made military glory their ideal.   They have regarded war, not like Treitschke and his school, as wholesome and necessary, but as an evil, an evil which, although it gives an opportunity (as Europe sees to-day) for splendid displays of patriotism and heroic valour, is the cause of infinite suffering and misery, and ought, if possible, to be got rid of from the world. The killing of workers and the destruction of property appear to them to be a hideous waste of human effort.   They have always been ready to fight when fighting became necessary.   But they have not, like Prussia, loved war for its own sake, for they believe that it has done more than anything else to retard the progress of mankind.

Our English ideal for the future is of a world in which every people shall have within its own borders a free national government resting on, and conforming to, the general will of its citizens, respecting the freedom of the individual, and not seeking to cramp or supersede his initiative, a government able to devote its efforts to improving the condition of the people without encroaching on its neighbours or putting unfair pressure upon them, or being disturbed by the fear of an attack from enemies abroad. Legislators and administrators have already tasks sufficiently difficult in reconciling the claims of different classes, in adjusting the interests of capital and labour, in promoting health and diffusing education and enlightenment, without the addition of those tasks and dangers which arise from the terror of foreign war.

There is, of course, a certain chauvinistic element in England, as in all countries, which finds some expression in newspapers and books. There are some persons with a deficient respect for the rights of other nations — persons who indulge in sentiments of hatred, persons who believe in force, persons who, in fact, have what is now known as the " Prussian view of the world," and the Prussian preference of Might to Right. But such persons are in Britain comparatively few; they are a diminishing quantity and they command little influence. The great bulk of the nation does not cherish hatreds, is satisfied with what it possesses, does not intend to aggress on its neighbours, does not seek to impose its own type of civilization on the world. Our English phrase " Live and let live " expresses this feeling. Though we prefer our own way of living for ourselves, we do not think it therefore the best for other peoples also, and no more wish to see the world all English than we wish to see it all Prussian.

The British people did not enter the war for the sake of gaining anything for themselves. They have not now fixed their mind on gaining (so far as concerns objects specially dear to themselves [1]) anything

<hr />

[1] I speak, of course, only of what regards Britain's own aims, not of those which primarily concern her Allies. Besides these aims there are, of course,

except a vindication of the sanctity of treaties, a completer security for the rights of neutral nations, the liberation of Belgium with full compensation to her for the injuries inflicted by the German armies, and adequate guarantees of future peace for themselves and their colonies. To this one must now add — since the Asiatic massacres of 1915 — measures that will make impossible in the future cruelties and oppressions such as the Turks have practised upon the Eastern Christians. They have been horrified by those massacres; and the disclosure of the plans of the German Government for obtaining control over Western Asia, including the Caucasian countries and Persia, have convinced them that neither Turks nor Germans can be suffered to retain any foothold east or south of the Taurus mountains.

In the foregoing pages I have sought to describe what I believe to be the principles and feelings and aims of the British people as a whole. It will not, I hope, be supposed that the description is submitted in a spirit of pharisaic self-satisfaction or self-assertion. We must not claim for Britain either that she is virtuous above other peoples, or that she has steadily lived up to her ideals. She has — as represented by her rulers — doubtless — sometimes declined from those ideals; and even since her Government became in 1832 more democratic, may have seemed from time to time oblivious of them, whether through passion and pride or in ignorance of facts which she ought to have known. Nevertheless the principles above set forth have been, in the main, those which have long guided her course at home, and have, more recently, guided also her policy abroad. They are the principles to which the na-

also to be regarded the questions which affect subject nationalities, now oppressed, and the questions which concern the welfare of native races, particularly in Africa.

tional mind has returned after temporary aberrations.
They are certainly those which animate her now, and
which are moving her to make sacrifices as great as a
people has ever made in what it held to be a righteous
cause.

Let me now add a few words of a more personal kind
to explain the sentiments of those Englishmen who
have in time past known and admired the achievements
of the German people in literature, learning, and science, who had desired peace with them, who had been
the constant advocates of friendship between the two
nations. Such Englishmen, who do not cease to be
lovers of peace because this war, felt to be righteous,
commands their hearty support, are now just as determined as any others to carry on the war to victory.
Why? Because to them this war presents itself as a
conflict of principles. On the one side there is the
doctrine that the end of the State is Power, that Might
makes Right, that the State is above morality, that
war is necessary and even desirable as a factor in
progress, that the rights of small States must give way
to the interests of great States, that the State may disregard all obligations whether undertaken by treaties
or prescribed by the common sentiment of mankind,
and that what is called military necessity justifies every
kind of harshness and cruelty in war. This is an old
doctrine — as old as the Sophists whom Socrates en-
countered in Athens. It has in every age been held
by some ambitious and unscrupulous statesmen. Many
a Greek tyrant of antiquity, many an Italian tyrant in
the Middle Ages and the Renaissance, put it in practice. Caesar Borgia is the most striking instance in
the fifteenth century, Philip II. of Spain and his min-
ions in the sixteenth, Frederick the Great in the eighteenth, Napoleon Bonaparte in the nineteenth.

On the other side there is the doctrine that the end
of the State is Justice, the doctrine that the State is,
like the individual, subject to a moral law and bound in
honour to observe its promises, that nations owe duties
to one another and to mankind at large, that they have
all more to gain by peace than by strife, that national
hatreds are deadly things, condemned by philosophy
and by Christianity.   In the victory of one or the other
of these two sets of principles the future of mankind
seems to us to be at stake.

I do not mean to attribute to the German people an
adherence to the former set of doctrines, for I do not
know how far these doctrines are held outside the
military and naval caste which has now unhappily
gained control of German policy, and it is hard to believe that the German people, as they were known to
those of us who studied at German universities more
than fifty years ago, could possibly approve of the action of their Government if their Government suffered
them to become acquainted with the facts relating to
the origin and conduct of the war as those facts are
now patent to the rest of the world.   As we English
had no hatred of the German people, neither have we
any wish to break up Germany, destroying her national
unity, or to take from her any territory which is really
German, or to interfere in any way with her internal
politics.   Our quarrel is with the German Government.
We think it a danger to every peaceful country, and
believe that in fighting against its doctrines, its ambitions, its methods of warfare, we and our Allies are
virtually fighting the battle of all peace-loving neutral
nations as well as our own.   We must fight on till
victory is won, for a Government which scorns treaties
and wages an inhuman warfare against innocent non-
combatants cannot be suffered to prevail by such meth-

ods. A triumphant and aggressive Germany, mistress of the seas as well as of the land, would be a menace to every nation, even to those of the western hemisphere. Had she been able to retain Belgium, to ruin France, to dominate Turkey and Persia and Turkistan, and, having done all this, to proceed to create an overwhelming navy — aims which it now appears she has cherished — adding to them that of exploiting Russia through vassal States in Finland, Esthonia, Lithuania, Poland, the Ukraine and Transcaucasia, no country would have been safe, not even Brazil and Argentina.

Be this as it may, the facts show that the present rulers of Germany have acted upon the former set of doctrines (already described) as consistently as ever did Frederick or Napoleon. They seem to us to be smitten with a kind of mental disease which has sapped honour, extinguished pity, and destroyed the sense of right and wrong. They invaded Belgium without provocation, and slaughtered thousands of innocent non-combatants. They persisted, against the protests of the United States, in drowning innocent non-combatants at sea. They looked calmly on while the Turkish allies whom they have dragged into the war, and whose action they could have restrained if they had cared to do so, were exterminating, with every cruelty Turkish ferocity can devise, a whole Christian nation. These things are a reversion to the ancient methods of savagery which marked the warfare of bygone ages. They are a challenge to civilized mankind — to neutrals as well as to the now belligerent States. Neutral nations would do well to recognize this, for they are themselves concerned. The same methods may be hereafter used against them as are being used now. They also ought to desire the defeat of any and every

Government which adopts such principles and practises such methods, for its victory would be a blow to morality and human progress which it would take centuries to retrieve.

Those Englishmen whose views I am seeking to express, recognizing the allegiance we all owe to humanity at large, and believing that progress is achieved more by co-operation than by strife, are hoping and striving for something more than the victory of their own country. They desire to see the world relieved from the burden of armaments and from that constant terror of war which has been darkening its sky for so many generations. They ask whether it may not be possible, after the war has come to an end, to form among the nations an effective League of Peace, embracing smaller as well as larger peoples, under whose aegis disputes might be amicably settled and the power of the League invoked to prevent any one State from disturbing the general tranquillity. The obstacles in the way of creating such a League are many and obvious, but whatever else may come out of the war, we in England hope that one result of it will be the creation of some machinery calculated to avert the recurrence of so awful a calamity as that from which mankind is now suffering. And this is one of the chief objects for which we are now contending, sacrificing every month thousands of the flower of our youth.

CHAPTER III

THE WAR STATE: ITS MIND AND ITS METHODS

THE present war differs from all that have gone before it, not only in its vast scale and in the volume of misery it has brought upon the world, but also in the fact that it is a war of Principles, and a war in which the permanent interests, not merely of the belligerent powers, but of all nations, are involved as such interests were never involved before. It concerns the world as a whole in both ways. The principles involved affect all mankind, but whichever way the issue of the war settles them, the settlement will be decisive for a long time to come. The good or evil fortune, materially and morally, of every nation, even of half-civilized tribes in Asia and Africa, will depend on the hands to whom power may fall when the war is over.

These are facts which many persons in neutral countries have not yet understood. In particular, they have not realized what are the doctrines and the ideals of the contending nations as these have appeared in the conduct of the war. Each side has proclaimed its doctrines and its ideals to some extent even in official documents, but far more fully through books and newspapers. Never before did belligerents make such efforts to put their respective cases before the world; never was the behaviour of the fighting forces the subject of so much comment. Nevertheless, in many neutral countries men seem to think that, as has usually happened in previous wars, there is no great distinction

between the combatants. They perceive that charges
and countercharges are bandied to and fro, and they
have not the patience to inquire which are true and
which false. Being perhaps too lazy or indifferent to
examine the motives and the conduct of the parties, they
lapse into the easy assumption that both are equally to
blame, and that if they themselves have any duty at all
as citizens of a neutral country, that duty is only to do
their best to bring back peace at the earliest possible
moment, with no thought for a more distant future.
Some neutral writers have put this view crudely by say-
ing it is only a quarrel of two dogs over a bone whom
the bystander would like to separate. Each nation is,
they assume, fighting for its own selfish interests, just as
the monarchs of Europe used to fight in the seventeenth
and eighteenth centuries to acquire territory or trade.

Now this is not such a war. I do not deny that such
a war of the older type might still occur. Nations
might quarrel over their respective territorial claims
and become angry enough to fight the matter out instead
of going to arbitration. Such a war need not have
raised any moral issue. For each of the contending
claims there might have been good arguments, and it
might well have been thought that faults on both sides
had led to the outbreak of hostilities. Even if the balance of merits inclined one way or the other, dispassion-
ate and well-informed observers in neutral countries
might have been divided in opinion as to those merits,
and have hesitated to express their sympathies, as
happened when war broke out between Prussia and
Austria in 1866 and again between Russia and Japan
in 1901.

But, let me repeat it, this is not a case in which neutrals can look on with an indifferent or merely curious
eye. This is a war of Principles, moral and political,

in which every man in neutral countries who has a sense of his personal duties to his own country, and to humanity, ought to try to find the truth and to form an honest and impartial judgment on the merits, so that the sentiment of his country may cast its weight on the side of what may appear to be that of Justice and of the general welfare.

Into the circumstances attending the outbreak of the war I will not here enter. That would lead me into too wide a field. Those circumstances may be studied in the documents published by the belligerent powers. No fuller and fairer examinations of them have been published than are contained in two books written by American jurists, the book of Professor Ellery Stowell entitled *The Diplomacy of the War of 1914,* and the book of Mr. James M. Beck called *The Evidence in the Case,* books to which rather than to any English book I desire to refer because their authors, being neutrals, wrote with a complete freedom from national bias. Since they appeared we have also had the Memorandum of Prince Lichnowsky.

I shall here examine, not the origins of the war, but the Conduct of the war, and that with especial reference to the light it casts upon the mind and purposes of those who rule Germany. However men may dispute as to the purposes and motives of the rulers and statesmen of Austria, Germany, Russia, France, and Britain, trying to set them in a worse or in a better light, the actual facts regarding the behaviour of the armed forces of the several nations are not really in dispute. Now and then some controversy has arisen about particular cases. But the broad facts stand; and these facts are enough, when carefully considered, to indicate the temper and spirit of the contending nations, to show by what principles they are guided, and what results the affirmation of those principles by success is likely to have on the future conduct of nations to one another and the welfare of mankind.

Accordingly, without stopping to refute charges brought against Britain of having desired and planned this war, nor the supposed malicious scheme of " encircling Germany " by a ring of enemies which has been falsely attributed to King Edward VII., I will go straight to the first act in the war, the invasion of Belgium.   It is a long-settled rule of international law that no belligerent nation has any right to claim a passage for its army across the territory of a neutral state; and the neutrality of Belgium had been guaranteed by a treaty signed in 1839 to which France, Prussia, and Great Britain were parties.   Nevertheless the position which Belgium held between the German Empire and France had obliged her to consider the possibility that in the event of a war between these two Powers her neutrality might not be respected.   That neutrality she was bound to maintain.   It was the condition of her creation and her existence.   So, in July 1914, when the danger of war between Germany and France seemed imminent, France and Germany were both asked by Belgium to renew their promises to abstain from violating her neutrality.   France promised.   The German Minister in Brussels replied that he knew of the assurances given by the German Chancellor in 1911 to respect Belgian neutrality, and that he " was certain that the sentiments expressed at that time had not changed." Nevertheless on August 2 the same Minister presented a note to the Belgian Government demanding a passage through Belgium for the German army on pain of an instant declaration of war.   Startled as they were by the suddenness with which this terrific war-cloud had risen on the eastern horizon, the leaders of the nation rallied round the king in his resolution to refuse the demand and to prepare for resistance. They were aware of the danger which would confront the civilian population of the country if it were tempted to take part in the work of national defence. Orders were accordingly issued by the civil governors of provinces, and by the burgomasters of towns, that the civilian inhabitants were to take no part in hostilities and to offer no provocation to the invaders. That no excuse might be furnished for severities, the populations of many important towns were instructed to surrender all firearms into the hands of the local officials. On the evening of August 4 the German armies crossed the frontier into Belgium. They immediately began to shoot harmless civilians and to set fire to villages. This was the opening of that campaign of slaughter and destruction which they carried on against the civilian population of this neutral and practically defenceless country, men, women, and children, for several weeks, till all Belgium, except a district in the south-west, had been subjugated.

All along the line of the German march innocent civilians, old men, women, and children, as well as other inhabitants, were murdered on the pretext that some persons in the towns and villages had shot at the invading force. The leading inhabitants — often priests — were constantly seized and called " hostages," who were to be put to death if any resistance was made by any civilian, though these persons were not responsible for such resistance and could not have prevented it. Such " hostages " were frequently shot.

Hundreds of innocent persons were seized, packed in baggage or cattle cars, and sent by railway to Germany, often without food or drink for many hours together. Villages and large parts of such a city as Louvain were destroyed by fire. Shocking outrages were committed upon women, and that by officers as well as soldiers, and little effort was made to restrain or punish such crimes, which were often committed under the influence of liquor.

The accounts of these murders and other excesses which the refugees who escaped from Belgium reported found at first little credence in England, for it was hard to believe that the soldiers of a civilized nation could commit them. But when the Belgian, French, and British Governments caused the evidence of eye-witnesses among the refugees to be carefully taken and tested, it was proved beyond all question not only that such things had happened, but that they had happened by the orders of the German officers, who themselves were acting under orders from headquarters, and who sometimes expressed regret at having to execute such orders. A full account of them, with many extracts from the evidence, will be found in the Reports issued by the Belgian Government and in the Report of the Committee appointed by the British Government, issued in May 1915.

If there are any persons in neutral countries who still think such things too horrible to be true, let them weigh these two facts. Diaries (written in German) found upon German prisoners or on the bodies of dead German soldiers contain records of the same (or quite similar) crimes as the evidence of the refugees established. The genuineness of these diaries, many of which have been published by the Belgian, French, and British investigators, is not disputed by the German Government. They alone are sufficient to prove how the troops behaved.

The second fact is that the German Government has never attempted to disprove the evidence adduced against them. They did publish an official reply to the

Belgian reports, but it consisted chiefly of allegations that Belgian civilians had given provocation by firing on German troops, thus " violating the well established rules of international law." As the German armies had entered Belgium in violation of international law, this argument loses whatever force it might have had if it had been engaged in legitimate warfare. But in point of fact the evidence adduced by the German White Book is often flimsy and untrustworthy, and the few cases with which it may be credited are conspicuously insufficient to justify, or even to palliate, the excesses committed by its troops. In reality, the vast majority of the persons executed, including the so-called " hostages," had no responsibility for the occasional firings, such as they may have been. The fact that some other civilian belonging to the same town may have fired on the invaders does not justify the killing of an innocent person. To seize innocent inhabitants, call them " hostages " for the good behaviour of their town, and shoot them if the invaders are molested by persons whose actions these so-called " hostages " cannot control, is murder and nothing else. Yet this is what the German commanders have done upon a great scale. The executions took place to strike terror into the Belgian population, to make easier the passage of the German armies, to coerce the Belgian forces into despair of resistance. This attempt at a justification was a tacit admission that the massacres had actually been perpetrated. The facts soon became known in Holland, a few miles from some of the towns where the worst atrocities had been perpetrated, and no one, outside Germany, now entertains any doubts regarding them.

These were the facts. What were the legal justifications put forward by the German Government?

Two were put forward. One was that France had

been planning to attack Germany through Belgium, and that French officers had, in pursuance of the plan, already entered Belgium to arrange for the execution of an offensive there. This was a pure invention. The story was improbable, for it was not in the military interests of France to adopt such a method, and no evidence was adduced to support it. It was soon dropped, having served its temporary purpose with the credulous German public.

The other allegation was that the British Government had conspired with that of Belgium sometime before to send a British army into the country to attack Germany. This was equally baseless. A British military attache had conversed with some Belgian officials as to what ought to be done if Germany were to invade Belgium, since Britain was pledged by a public treaty to defend Belgium in the event of her being attacked by any foreign power, a contingency which it was necessary to provide for, but no idea of making an offensive against Germany through her had ever been entertained in England; and this has been conclusively shown by the texts which the British Government has published. England had saved Belgian territory from attack in 1870 by requiring both France and Germany to abstain from entering it, and she might have to do so again. Bismarck and Louis Napoleon had then given the promise required, but England could not be sure that Bismarck's successors would do so likewise.

On this head, however, nothing more need be said, for the German Chancellor openly confessed in the Reichstag a few days after the beginning of the war that his Government had " committed a wrong " and had violated international law [1] by carrying war into a neutral country, the neutrality and independence of

1 The *German War Manual* itself recognizes this principle.

which they had guaranteed, and which, had there been
no guarantee at all, was entitled by international law,
and on the common principles of justice, to be exempt
from invasion. His plea was military necessity, a necessity of which Germany herself was to be the judge.

When the German armies entered France, they applied the same methods as in Belgium. Non-combatants were ruthlessly murdered. Villages were destroyed; houses pillaged and burnt. Women were
violated, and no attempt made to restrain either the
lust or the ferocity of the soldiery. Full accounts of
these horrors, confirmed by the evidence of many soldiers' diaries, have been published by the French Government, and others may be found in the British Committee's Reports, as well as in many books, such as that
of Professor Morgan.

Next after the murders on land came those at sea.
Submarines began to destroy, usually without any warning, unarmed merchant vessels, drowning their crews,
and also unarmed passenger vessels, drowning their
passengers. The *Lusitania,* in which nearly twelve
hundred people perished, many of them citizens of neutral countries, was only one of many cases. Fishing-
boats were constantly destroyed, and cases occurred in
which, when a vessel had been destroyed, its crew, trying
to escape, were shelled by the submarine, or the submarine placed them on its upper surface and then sub-
merged, drowning them. These practices, gross violations of the rule of international law, which requires
that the safety of those on board a merchant ship shall
be provided for if she is sunk, have gone on till now.
Even hospital ships, about whose character there could
be no mistake, have been frequently torpedoed.

Concurrently with these acts there were frequent
attacks upon open undefended coast towns in England,

often upon health resorts, such as Scarborough and Ramsgate, in which many civilians were killed.

A little later than the murders on land and sea came the murders from the air. In the many air-raids over England no military damage has been done, and only a handful of soldiers, about fifty (so far as I know), have suffered. But many hundreds of innocent civilians, mostly women and children, have been maimed or killed; and the murders still go on. The German Government must by this time know that these raids have no effect upon the British people except to rouse their anger and so to make them more determined than ever to prosecute the war. Such murders were blunders as well as crimes. Why, then, were the air-raids and the shelling of undefended coast towns continued? No military object was attained. Hardly any soldiers were killed. It was the civilians that suffered. The motive seems to have been to encourage the German people at home to believe that the English were being terrified, and to console them for the disappointments of military failure by the notion that in some way or other the German force was making itself effectively felt by the enemy they were being taught to hate.

Many particular instances of cruelty may be passed over. That of Miss Edith Cavell, the lady who was, while nursing in a hospital at Brussels, executed for having aided a refugee to escape, is well remembered. But that of Captain Fryatt deserves mention, because he was vindictively put to death in cold blood, in flagrant violation of international law, for having, some months before a German vessel took him prisoner, gallantly defended the passenger vessel which he was commanding against the attack of a German submarine, such defence being entirely legitimate, and, as legitimate, part of his duty to his own country.

In 1916 a new series of cruelties began to be practised upon civilians. At Lille and other towns in Northern France occupied by German troops many hundreds of girls were torn from their homes and carried off to Germany to be set to forced labour there, some of them, no doubt, destined to experience an even worse fate. About the same time many thousands of Belgian working men were seized, and on the pretext that there was no employment for them in the towns where they lived, were carried off, amid the cries of their children and the shrieks of their wives, who flung themselves on the rails in front of the locomotives, to German towns, where they were forced to work for their enemy masters against their own fellow-countrymen.

The motive, so the German Government announced, was a philanthropic one. It is not good for workmen to loiter unemployed. They will be happier if they have something to do. The unemployment, it need hardly be said, had been caused by the German Government itself, which had taken out of the country for its own use all the raw materials of industry and all the machinery.

These workmen, though deprived of their former means of livelihood, were not starving. When the Germans refused to feed them, they were and had continued to be fed by the charity of Americans and Englishmen, directed by the admirable skill and energy of an American, Mr. Hoover. In one Belgian province, where some private factories were still going, the German authorities stopped these in order to invent a ground for treating the workmen as unemployed and driving them off into Germany to labour there. This is slave-raiding, worthy of those Arab marauders whom Livingstone tried to root out of Africa.[1]

1 As to these slave-raidings, see the book of M. Passelecy entitled, *Les de-*

A similar violation of the best settled rules of international law was carried out in Poland. Here the Polish inhabitants of the invaded districts which the German armies occupy were forced into the German Army on the pretext that the country had been already conquered and its people virtually German subjects. They were roped in and driven to die in order to perpetuate the tyranny which the German Government had already been exercising over their brethren in a part of old Poland which she has held by force these many years.

The facts here briefly enumerated are indisputable and undisputed facts. Whatever the excuses or palliations which the German Government may put forward, all these acts are flagrant violations, not only of the rules laid down by writers on international law, but of the long-settled practice of civilized nations.

They are even worse. They violate the fundamental principles of natural justice and of common humanity. Even Bonaparte, whose offences shocked his contemporaries, did not in eighteen years of war so offend against helpless innocence or commit so many breaches of the much laxer international rules of his time, nor as the German Generals have committed since August 4, 1914.

Last of all, I come to a case which surpasses all the others here mentioned or referred to, not only in the vastness of its scale, but in the hideous cruelties which were practised upon the victims, and in the fact that the victims did not belong to any of the countries with whom Germany was at war. They were the subjects, the innocent and helpless subjects, of one of Germany's trusted Allies. Among the peoples upon whom this

portations belges a la lumiere des documents Allemands, published at Paris and Nancy in 1917.

war has brought calamity and suffering, the Armenian people have had the most to endure.   Great as has been the misery inflicted upon Belgium and Northern France, upon Poland, upon Serbia, the misery of Armenia, though far less known to the outer world, has been far more terrible.

When the European War broke out in 1914, the government of the Turkish Empire had fallen into the hands of a small gang of unscrupulous ruffians calling themselves the Committee of Union and Progress, who were ruling through their command of the army, but in the name of the harmless and imbecile Sultan.   By means which have not yet been fully disclosed, but the nature of which can be easily conjectured,[1] this gang were won over to serve the interests of Germany; and at Germany's bidding they declared war against the Western Allies, thus dragging all the subjects of Turkey, Muslim and Christian, into a conflict with which they had no concern.   The Armenian Christians scattered through the Asiatic part of the Turkish dominions, having had melancholy experience in the Adana massacres some years previously of the cruelties which the Committee were capable of perpetrating, were careful to remain quiet, and to furnish no pretext to the Turkish authorities for an attack upon them.   But the masters of Turkey showed that they did not need any pretext for the execution of the purposes they cherished.[2]   They had formed a design for the extermination of the non-Mohammedan elements in the popula-

1 An extremely interesting account of the process by which the German Government lured the Turks into the war has been given by Mr. Morgenthau, who was then United States Ambassador at Constantinople, and had the best opportunities of watching the course of events, in the numbers for June and July of a well-known American magazine, *The World's Work.*

2 The evidence for what is here stated will be found in the Blue Book (Miscellaneous, No. 31 of 1916) entitled *The Treatment of Armenians in the Ottoman Empire, 1915-16,* published by the British Government. No attempt has been made to reply to it, though the Turkish authorities invented a few false stories alleging provocation by a few of the Christians.

tion of Asiatic Turkey, in order to make what they called a homogeneous nation, consisting of Mohammedans only. The wickedness of such a design was equalled only by its blind folly, for the Christian Armenians of Asia Minor and the north-eastern provinces constituted the most industrious, the most intelligent, and the best-educated part of the population. Most of the traders and merchants, nearly all the skilled artisans, were Armenians, and to destroy them was to destroy the best industrial asset which these regions possessed. However, this was the plan of the Committee of Union and Progress, and as soon as they began to feel, in the spring of 1915, that the Allied expedition against the Dardanelles was not likely to succeed, they proceeded to execute it. They first disarmed all the Armenians in order to have them at their mercy, frequently compelling by tortures the surrender of arms; and in some cases, in order to make it appear that the Armenians were intending to take up arms, they actually sent weapons into the towns and then had them seized as evidence against the Christians. When such means of defence as the Christians possessed had been secured, orders for massacre were issued from Constantinople to the local governors. The whole Armenian population was seized. The grown men were slaughtered without mercy.[1] The American Consul at Kharput saw the ravines in the mountains full of skeletons. Others have described the lines of corpses that lay along the roads for miles. The younger women were sold in the market-place to the highest bidder, or appropriated by Turkish military officers and civil officials to become slaves in Turkish harems. The boys were handed over to dervishes to be carried off and brought up as Mus-

[1] Some of the professors in the American colleges were murdered. So were several bishops: one was burnt alive.

lims. The rest of the hapless victims, all the older men and women, the mothers and their babes clinging to them, were torn from their homes and driven out along the tracks which led into the desert regions of northern Syria and Arabia. Most of them perished on the way from hardships, from disease, and from starvation. Some few have been rescued by the British officers in Mesopotamia. A few were still surviving in 1917 near Aleppo and along the banks of the Euphrates. Many, probably many thousands, were drowned in that river and its tributaries, martyrs to their Christian faith, which they had refused to renounce; for it was generally possible for women, and sometimes for men, to save themselves by accepting Mohammedanism. By these various methods hundreds of thousands — the number is variously estimated at from 600,000 to 800,000 — have perished. Germany claims to be a Christian country. Its Emperor and its ministers of religion are constantly representing themselves as the special objects of Divine favour and protection. Now the German Government knew what was going on. Their Consuls reported to them. Some of their missionaries besought them to stop the massacres, declaring that the name of Germany would be for ever disgraced if these horrors continued. But no step was taken to arrest the hand of the destroyer. Instead of arresting it, they have honoured the two chief criminals, Talaat and Enver, with many compliments, and have made the last named of these wretches a Colonel in the German army. All happened with the tacit acquiescence of the German Government, some of whose representatives on the spot were even said to have encouraged the Turks in their work of slaughter, while the Government confined its action to the propagation in Germany, so as to deceive its own people, false stories which alleged that the Armenians had been punished for insurrectionary movements, and to the exercise of a rigid censorship to prevent the truth from becoming known, through missionary accounts, to the German people.   They made themselves accessories, whether before the crime or after the crime, to the most awful catastrophe that has ever befallen a Christian nation.   Whether they desired to be rid of the most enterprising and vigorous race in Western Asia because it might be in the way of their plans for dominating those regions, or whether they merely desired to keep their friends of the Turkish gang in good humour by letting them kill to their hearts' content, we do not yet know.   Whichever was the motive, the result is the most signal illustration yet given of the lengths to which the doctrine of a State interest, standing high above all morality and all compassion, can be pushed.

All these facts, with many details too horrible to be repeated here, are set forth in the Blue Book recently published in England, based upon incontrovertible evidence, and to which no reply has been made, though some denials, palpably false, have emanated from the Turkish gang.

The case of Armenia is peculiarly instructive as regards the principles which guide the German Government, because it shows the civil authorities just as unscrupulous and just as ruthless as the chiefs of the army and navy.   Though the German Chancellor and the Foreign Secretary acquiesced in the invasion of Belgium, they doubtless saw the political objections.   One can well believe them to have remonstrated with the Emperor, but to have been overborne by the pressure of the soldiers.   The shifts to which the Chancellor was driven for excuses, and his too-frank relief of his conscience by the admission of wrongdoing, suggest a reluctance. But the acquiescence in and tacit approval of the Asiatic massacres was a matter which fell within the province of the civilians and the Ambassador at Constantinople, and they showed a want of conscience, or human feeling, of religious feeling, which the most nardened soldier could not have surpassed.

These are, presented in the barest outline, the essential facts regarding the conduct of this war by the German Government and its military chiefs. Be it noted that the acts done were not done at random. They were not due to the brutality of individual officers or the passion of excited soldiers. They were done on principle, in pursuance of a settled policy. Said a German officer at Brussels: " I have not done one-hundreth part of what I have been ordered to do by the High German military authorities." [1] The crimes perpetrated happened — as the British Committee observe in their Report (p. 43) —" not from mere military licence, for the discipline of the German army is proverbially stringent, and its obedience implicit. Not from any special ferocity of the troops, for whoever has travelled among the German peasantry knows that they are as kindly and good-natured as any people in Europe. The excesses recently committed in Belgium were, moreover, too widespread and too uniform in their character to be mere sporadic outbursts of passion or rapacity. The explanation seems to be that these excesses were committed — in some cases ordered, in others allowed — on a system and in pursuance of a set purpose. That purpose was to strike terror into the civil population and dishearten the Belgian troops, so as to crush down resistance and extinguish the very

---

1 Report of the British Committee, p. 42. Other instances are given, in which officers regretted the acts which their orders compelled them to do. There are doubtless plenty of naturally humane men in the German army, and that makes their subjection to the detestable system all the more regrettable.

spirit of self-defence." This is evidently applicable
also to the acts of inhumanity perpetrated by the cap-
tains of the German submarines, when they killed, by
shooting or by drowning, the crews of boats they cap-
tured. They wished to terrorize British sailors, and
nothing in the war has reflected more credit on any
class of men than the fact that British sailors and fisher-
men were not terrorized.

The German manual of military practice (*Kriegs-
buch im Landkriege*) goes a long way to justify these
acts, for it recognizes as proper the taking and, if necessary, killing of hostages, the killing of a non-combatant
who, being compelled to guide the troops of an enemy,
leads them wrong. It declares that war must be directed against "the whole intellectual and moral resources of the enemy country" and not merely against
the combatant armies. It even goes so far as to hint
that "the exploitation of the crimes of third parties
(assassination, robbery, incendiarism, and the like) is
not opposed to international law." It bids an officer
"to guard himself against excessive humanitarian notions." It advises him to study in military history the
instances of stern severity. But, shocking as many of
its propositions are, it condemns many particular offences of which the German officers were constantly
guilty, and which were committed, as the evidence
proves by the orders of the High Command, as part of
their regular system. Its doctrine that military necessity (*Kriegsnoth*) is a general warrant for any sort of
action was carried out by them even where their Manual seemed to recognize restrictions.

These facts, considered and remembered, make a sad
and terrible catalogue, which we would all gladly forget, but it needs to be presented for two reasons. One
is that it furnishes materials from which neutral nations

may form a judgment as to the ideas and characters of
the belligerent Governments, apart altogether from
those questions relating to the original merits of the
quarrel round which controversy still rages.   Whatever
may have been the motives and intentions of the German Government, here are its acts, unrepented of, justified as a necessary part of war.   Let neutrals judge
from them, comparing them with the behaviour of the
armies and fleets of the Entente Powers, what the triumph of one or other of the belligerent groups is likely
to mean for the future peace and welfare of the world.

The other reason is to enable the peoples of the
Entente States and of America, as well as the neutral
peoples, to understand the difficulties which surround
the making of a treaty of peace with a Government
which has such a record.

For what is it that the facts here summarized prove?
They show, and the German War Manual shows:

1. That the German Government, by its own avowal,
   does not respect treaties when State interests
   require them to be broken.

2. That it does not observe any engagements it has
   made regarding methods of conducting war.
   Most, perhaps all, of those it made at Hague
   Conferences have been violated.

3. That it draws little, if any, distinction in the conduct of war between combatants and non-
   combatants.

4. That it shows, not only no sense of what used to
   be called " chivalry " in war, but no sense of
   pity for the helpless and the suffering.

5. That it directs, or at least encourages, the inflic-
   tion of the wanton destruction of property and
   objects of beauty or historic interest, where no

military advantage, unless that of terroriza-
tion, is to be expected.

6. That its only rule of action is to follow every
method, however inhuman, however illegal,
that is calculated to attain success.

How are we to explain the proclamation of such
doctrines and the carrying out of them in practice by
the Government of a great nation which has attained,
at various epochs of its long history, so much distinction
in, and rendered such services to, philosophy and science, literature and art?

The explanation lies partly in the history of Prussia,
the state which has, since 1870, dominated and moulded
the mind of Germany. It is a history of success in and
by War from the end of the seventeenth century. It
was observed long ago that the trade of Prussia is War.
Among them the Soldier is the Master. Professor
Gilbert Murray has excellently said: —

Germany has produced the specialized soldier, not the humane
soldier, the Christian soldier, the chivalrous soldier, or the soldier with a sense of civil duties, but the soldier who is trained
to be a soldier and nothing else, to disregard all the rest of
human relations, to see all his country's neighbours merely as
enemies to be duped and conquered, to see all life according to
some system of perverted biology as a mere struggle of force
and fraud. The Germans have created this type of soldier,
alike concentrated, conscienceless, and remorseless, and then —
what no other people in the world has done — they have given
the nation over to his guidance.

This worship of War would not have spread from
the military class throughout the nation had it not been
accompanied by and blent with a worship of the State.
It is the German conception of the State as an all-
mastering power, to which every subject must conse-
crate all his talents and activities, that has created
among the people a sort of war idolatry. Militarism,

instead of being restrained or softened down by the thinkers, the men of learning and science, has been allowed to infuse its poison into the mind of the nation, the nation being, one must remember, a nation in arms, and the army the nation. The British Committee, expressing their amazement at the doctrines held and put in practice by the German High Command, observe (p. 44) : —

In the minds of Prussian officers War seems to have become a sort of sacred mission, one of the highest functions of the omnipotent State, which is itself as much an Army as a State. Ordinary morality and the ordinary sentiment of pity vanish in its presence, superseded by a new standard which justifies to the soldier every means that can conduce to success, however shocking to a natural sense of justice and humanity, however revolting to his own feelings. The Spirit of War is deified. Obedience to the State and its War Lord leaves no room for any other duty or feeling. Cruelty becomes legitimate when it promises victory. Proclaimed by the heads of the army, this doctrine would seem to have permeated the officers and affected even the private soldiers, leading them to justify the killing of non-combatants as an act of war, and so accustoming them to slaughter that even women and children become at last the victims. It cannot be supposed to be a national doctrine, for it neither springs from nor reflects the mind and feelings of the German people as they have heretofore been known to other nations. It is a specifically military doctrine, the outcome of a theory held by a ruling caste who have brooded and thought, written and talked and dreamed about War until they have fallen under its obsession and been hypnotized by its spirit.

It is a singular result of this kind of obsession that it may affect the normal working of the mind in matters outside the sphere with which the mind is chiefly and primarily occupied. In the case of the German military caste, it prevented them from seeing and comprehending the political facts with which, in the pursuit of their military aims, they had to deal. They did not

perceive that the outer world would not recognize what
had become to them fundamental axioms. They did
not foresee that ruthlessness and faithlessness would
rouse against them an anger and hatred which would do
them a harm in the field of politics exceeding whatever
gain ruthlessness and faithlessness could bring them in
the field of war. Bishop Butler once asked whether a
nation could go mad. The distortion of the military
mind from the natural human view of things so disturbed its balance as to produce something resembling
monomania.

As it is hard to describe the German worship of the
State, except in terms drawn from religion, so the nearest parallel to this obsession of a highly trained body
of men by one dominant idea, which extinguishes ordinary morality and normal human feeling, is to be found
in the fanaticism which occasionally seizes those who
have come to live in one doctrine and for one purpose,
which becomes their faith. The Spanish Inquisitors of
the sixteenth century were possessed by a zeal for orthodoxy which narrowed their minds to a single conception of life and duty. The one thing that mattered was
to bring and keep every human creature to the words
and forms of the orthodox Roman creed and worship.
Heresy was the deadliest thing in the world, for only by
exact orthodoxy and implicit obedience to the Church
could souls be saved. This belief covered their whole
sky; this extinguished all other feelings. They were
not naturally worse than other men. But to them all
methods were lawful for tracking down a heretic, all
cruelties laudable that could extort a confession or the
disclosure of an accomplice, or could give to punishment a more frightfully deterrent power. Strange are
the aberrations of human nature. Fanaticism may
manifest itself in one sphere of thought and action or

another.   But its familiar symptoms always recur; and
they may be as deadly in the soldier as in the priest.

We may now revert to the practical issues which this
study of German war methods raises for neutral nations.   What help does it afford them for judging the
questions involved in the conflict which the Entente
Powers on the one hand, Germany and Austria on the
other, are maintaining?   What light does it throw on
the characters of the belligerent nations themselves?

We have seen what Germany's war doctrines are and
how perfectly her practice follows and conforms to her
doctrines.   Can any charges similar to those which have
been proved against her be advanced against the armies
or the fleets of Britain, France, and Italy?   Have they
broken faith or murdered non-combatants, or gone in
any respect beyond what the settled rules for the conduct of war authorize?   It may be that here and there
regrettable acts have been done by individual soldiers.
Such things cannot but happen in any war.   But the
military and naval authorities have, as everybody
knows — except, indeed, the German people, who have
been fed up by their Government with false stories
against French soldiers and British sailors — conducted
their operations with as much regard to justice and
humanity as the process of fighting allows, and have
abstained from severities which the doctrine of Retalia-
tion upon an enemy who has himself violated international usage might have allowed.   No maxims of
cruelty, no justifications of it as necessary, like those
which the German Manual contains, stand in the books
used by British officers for their guidance.   If, therefore, a verdict is to be delivered by neutrals upon the
merits of this war after a consideration of the way in
which it has been actually waged, can they have any
doubt as to the side that is entitled to their sympathy?

If they look into the future and ask themselves what
will be the effect on the welfare of mankind which the
victory of one or other party in such a conflict of principles, principles only too well illustrated by practice,
must have, have they not ample materials for their decision? Let them ask themselves what difference will it
make to the world if the War doctrines and State doctrines maintained by the German Government are approved by success, and if German war methods are
found to have accomplished what the High Command
expects from them?

Through many centuries the nations have been slowly
climbing out of the savagery of primitive tribal warfare
into the general acceptance and observance of rules for
the conduct of war which, if they did not remove, did at
least mitigate its horrors, and limited their range by
assuring safety to non-combatants. The German Government has now gone back to savagery. All restrictions are removed. All pretence of good faith is tossed
aside. If Germany should win the war the stamp of
success will have been set upon her methods. She will
reproduce them and other nations will imitate them in
those future wars which her scientific thinkers pronounce
to be necessary for the progress of mankind. The
gains of these later centuries will have been lost, and
the last state of the world will have become so much
worse than the first, because the evil spirits that had
seemed to have been exorcised will now have at their
command the boundless resources of modern science.

There is another feature of the war and of the part
which the German Government has been playing in it
which may give cause for thought to those neutral peoples that value liberty. Respect for the Rights of Man
as Man is the foundation of every free self-governing
community. If therefore any State shows itself in war

disregardful of human rights in the person of civilian non-combatants, as, for instance, if it murders or enslaves them, it commits what may be called a political as well as a moral offence, indicating its scorn for those feelings, and trampling on the laws and customs which hold communities together.   Whatever brings back the régime of brute force lowers human nature and destroys men's confidence in one another.   Right and Duty are the cement which holds citizens together in a free commonwealth.   A blow struck at them is a blow struck at democracy.

Another question also is raised which affects not only neutrals, but also the peoples of the Entente countries and of the United States.   When the time arrives for negotiating a peace — and it must be a peace whose conditions are not left to the discretion of the Governments, but one approved by the will of the peoples — what principles, what considerations are to prescribe their action in settling the terms to be given to a defeated Germany?

I pass by the preliminary difficulty on which many writers and speakers have dwelt — that of making a treaty with a Government which has announced that it does not respect treaties any further or longer than suits its own interests, but will break its promises when State necessity requires.   The difficulty is a real one. Treaties, however, must be made, though the experience of Belgium may suggest that the performance of their obligations will need to be fortified by something stronger than a scrap of paper.

A further feature of the situation is unfortunate. The behaviour of the German armies in France and Belgium, the murders of American and English non-combatants by the German submarines, the inhumanity with which prisoners of war have been treated — all these things have evoked a cry for revenge. That was inevitable. But revenge, however natural, is a bad guide in politics. The more it can be held in check, the better for the victors themselves.

In the peace congresses heretofore held the questions discussed have usually turned upon material interests, such as cessions of territory or war indemnities, or future conditions of trade, or possibly upon the protection of subject populations, such as were the Christian subjects of Turkey or (in former days) the Protestant subjects of Roman Catholic Powers. But this war presents some different phenomena. It is a war of Principles, a war between two hostile systems of ideas. These systems are irreconcilable. One of them has challenged the other to a mortal combat. If it is not defeated it may be expected to renew that combat so soon as it has recovered from that exhaustion which awaits all the combatants. The interests involved are not material merely. They are also moral.

Victory will consist not merely in such territorial re-arrangements as the principle of nationality, judiciously applied, may show to be needed for the future peace of Europe and Western Asia (including, of course, the liberation of Belgium and Serbia and the deliverance of the Eastern Christians from the Turks), but also in assuring the triumph of the principles which are at stake, and which have brought Britain and America into the war, the respect for the faith of treaties, and for the rights of small nations, the protection of non-combatants in war, the overthrow of what is called Prussian Militarism, that system whose unbridled ambition has threatened the liberties of the world.

Every thoughtful man, every one who has any pity in his heart, must desire this war, which has been destroying the flower of our youth and carrying sorrow into every home, to be brought to a speedy end. But we must also feel — and those of us who have been workers for peace through all our lives feel it as much as any others — that a peace made now, leaving the military system and military caste of Germany still unbroken in power, in credit, in self-confidence, in its prestige and ascendancy over its own people, would be only a truce, a brief respite in a conflict which that military caste would resume as soon as it had repaired its losses.

To make the sort of treaty which the German Government desires, and which it from time to time hints it might accept, would not only leave that Government in possession of ill-gotten gains, with no adequate reparation for the wrongs it has inflicted, but would be an acquiescence in, almost an encouragement to repeat, the methods by which its armies has carried on the war, and would leave the peace-loving peoples the victims to perpetually recurring fears and suspicions, obliged to maintain military and naval armaments even vaster and costlier than those which had become, before the war, an intolerable burden. The Allies feel, and they desire neutral nations to know, that if it becomes necessary to fight on till the ill-gotten gains have been disgorged and the reparation made, neither passion nor revenge, but a conviction of what is needed for future safety will be their motive.

What, then, can be done to overthrow what is called " Prussian Militarism "? There is no more use in reasoning with the military caste that rules Germany than there would have been in reasoning with Spanish Inquisitors. Their premises, the settled convictions by which they are possessed and obsessed, are fundamentally different from those which the Western nations hold. Whatever Christianity may mean to them, it means something different from what it means to us in

Britain and America. Who their God is we know not. He is not our God. Can we appeal to the German people? Unfortunately a large part of the educated upper class would seem to have been either indoctrinated with militaristic doctrines or debarred by national patriotism from expressing open dissent. The masses of the people have been kept in ignorance of the causes of the war and the real behaviour of their rulers. They have formed habits of obedience, and they have not the constitutional means that democracies possess for asserting their will and changing the policy of the Government. We have hoped and waited for an assertion of that will, but so far we have waited in vain. It is not for us to interfere with the internal affairs of Germany. "Who would be free, themselves must strike the blow."

These things being so, the only course left would seem to be to cut up by its roots the cause which has given to Prussian militarism the power over the German mind which it enjoys. That cause has been the long tradition of military victory, and of the extension and enrichment of the State by war. If this military prestige can be destroyed, the power of the ruling caste will wither and fall. The British and American peoples ought not to wish, and I believe that they do not wish, to dismember Germany or to inflict any permanent injury on her people. What they seek is a peace of safety, a peace the terms of which shall make it clear to the world, and especially to the German people, that the doctrine of Force as the only power, and the practice of those methods by which Force has been applied, have been decisively condemned by Failure, and that the most tremendous effort ever made to substitute Force for Right has been defeated, because it evoked the righteous indignation of the world.

CHAPTER IV

WAR AND HUMAN PROGRESS

*An Address delivered on the Huxley Foundation to the University of
Birmingham in 1916*

I

THOSE who have studied the general principles that
guide human conduct, and the working out of these
principles as recorded in history, have noted two main
streams of tendency. One of these tendencies shows
itself in the power of Reason and of those higher and
gentler altruistic emotions, which the development of
Reason or Philosophy as the guide of life tends to
evoke and foster. The other tendency is associated
with the less rational elements in man — with passion
and those self-regarding impulses which attain their
ends by physical violence.

Thus two schools of philosophical thinkers or historians have been formed. One lays stress on the
power of the former set of tendencies. It finds in
them the chief sources of human progress in the past,
and expects from them its further progress in the
future. It regards men as capable of a continual advance through the increasing influence of reason and
sympathy. It dwells on the ideas of Justice and Right
as the chief factors in the amelioration of society, and
therefore regards good-will and peace as the goal of
human endeavour in the sphere both of national and of
international life. Its faith in human nature — that

72

is to say, in the possibility of improving human nature — fills it with hopes for the ordinary man, who may, in its view, be brought by education, and under a régime of beneficence, to a higher level than he has yet anywhere attained.

The other school is less sanguine. It insists on the power of selfishness and of passion, holding these to be elements in human action which can never be greatly refined or restrained, either by reason or by sympathy. Social order — so it holds — can be secured only by Force, and Right itself is created only by Force. It is Force that has in the past made what men call Right and Law and Government; it is still Force alone that sustains the social structure. The average man needs discipline; and the best thing he can do is to submit to the strong man — strength, of course, consisting not only in physical capacity, but in a superiority of will and intellect also. This school, which used to defend slavery as useful and, indeed, necessary — the older among us can remember a time when that ancient, time-honoured institution was still so defended — prefers the rule of the superior One or Few, *i.e.* monarchy or oligarchy, to the rule of the Many. Quite consistently, it has usually regarded war as a necessary and valuable form of discipline, because war is the final embodiment and test of physical force.

This opposition can be traced a long way back. It is already visible in the days of Plato, who combats the teaching of some of the Sophists that Justice is merely the advantage of the strong. From his time onward great philosophical schools followed his lead. So the poets, from Hesiod onward, gave an ideal expression to the joys of peace in their pictures of a Golden Age before the use of copper and iron had been discovered. Virgil describes the primeval *Saturnia Regna,* the time

before war trumpets were blown or the anvil sounded
under the strokes of the swordsmith's hammer:

> Necdum etiam audierant inflari classica, necdum
> Impositos duris crepitare incudibus enses.

This was the happy time of man, to which the Roman
poet who acclaimed the restoration of peace by Augustus looked back, desiring a rest from the unending
strife of the ancient world. Just after Virgil's day,
Christianity proclaimed peace as its message to all
mankind. Twelve hundred years later, in an age full
of strife, Dante, the most imaginative mind of the
Middle Ages, hoped for peace from the universal sway
of a pious and disinterested Emperor; and, nearly six
hundred years after him, in the days of Frederick the
Great of Prussia, Immanuel Kant, the greatest meta-
physician of the modern world, produced his plan for
the establishment of an everlasting peace.

These hopes and teachings of poets and philosophers, though they had little power in the world of fact
(for few rulers or statesmen, even of those who rendered lip-service to pacific principles, ever tried to apply
them to practice), continued to prevail in the world
of theory, and seemed, especially after the final extinction of slavery half a century ago and the spread
of democracy from America to Europe, to be passing
into the category of generally accepted truths.

Latterly, however, there has come a noteworthy reaction. A school of thinkers has arisen which, not
content with maintaining war to be a necessary factor
in the relations between states, as being the only ultimately available method of settling their disputes, declares it to be a method in itself wholesome and socially
valuable. To these thinkers it is not an inevitable evil,
but a positive good — a thing not merely to be expected

and excused, but to be desired for the benefits it confers
on mankind.   This school challenges the assumptions
of the lovers of peace and denounces their projects of
disarmament and arbitration as pernicious.   War, it
seems, is a medicine which human society needs, and
which must be administered at frequent intervals; for
it is the only tonic capable of bracing up the character
of a nation.

Such doctrines are a natural result of the system of
thought which exalts the functions and proclaims the
supremacy of the State.   The State stands by Power.
The State is Power.   Its power rests upon force.   By
force it keeps order and executes the law within its
limits.   Outside its limits there is no law, but only
force.   Neither is there any morality.   The State is a
law unto itself, and owes no duty to other states.   Self-
preservation is the principle of its being.   Its Might
is Right, the only possible Right.   War, or the threat
of war, is the sole means by which the State can make
its will prevail against other states; and where its interest requires war, to war it must resort, reckless of
the so-called rights of others.

This modern doctrine, or rather this modernized
and developed form of an old doctrine, bases itself on
two main arguments.   One is drawn from the realm
of animated nature, the other from history.   Both lines
of argument are meant to show that all progress is
achieved by strife.   Among animals and plants it is
Natural Selection and the Struggle for Life that have
evolved the higher forms from the lower, destroying
the weaker species, and replacing them by the stronger.
Among men it is the same process of unending conflict
that has enabled the higher races and the more civilized
states to overcome the lower and less advanced, either
extinguishing them altogether, or absorbing them and

imposing upon such of them as remain, the more perfect type of the conquerors.

The theory I am describing has, in these latest years,
acquired for us a more than theoretical interest.   It
has passed out of the world of thought into the world
of action, becoming a potent factor in the relations of
states.   It has been used to justify, not merely war
itself, but methods of warfare till recently unheard
of — methods which, though recommended as promoting human progress, threaten to carry us back into the
ages of barbarism.   It deserves to be carefully ex-
amined, so that we may see upon what foundations it
rests.   I propose to consider briefly the two lines of
argument just referred to, which may be called the biological and the historical.

II

Never yet was a doctrine adopted for one set of reasons which its advocates could not somehow contrive
to support by other reasons.   In the Middle Ages
men generally resorted to the Bible, rarely failing to
find a text which they could so interpret as to justify
their views or their acts.   Pope Gregory the Seventh,
perhaps the most striking figure of the eleventh century, proved to the men of his time that his own spiritual power was superior to the secular power by citing
that passage in the Book of Genesis which says that
the sun was created to rule the day and the moon to
rule the night.   The modern reader may not see the
connection, but Gregory's contemporaries did.   The
sun was the Popedom and the moon was the Empire.
In our own time — I am old enough to remember the
fact, and the reader will find it referred to in *Uncle
Tom's Cabin,* a book which ought to be still read, for
its appearance was followed by great results — the

apologists of Negro slavery justified that " peculiar institution " by quoting the passage in Genesis where Noah prophesies that Ham, or rather Canaan the son of Ham, shall serve his elder brother Shem.   In the then current biblical ethnology, Ham was the progenitor of the black races of Africa, and the fact that even that ethnography did not make Shem the progenitor of the Anglo-American race, which the children of Ham were destined to serve, was passed lightly over.   This argument had no great currency outside the Slave States.   But another book besides the Bible was open, and to that also an appeal was made: the Book of Nature.   It was frequently alleged by the defenders of slavery in Europe, as well as in America, that the Negro was not really a man, but one of the higher apes, and certain points from his bone-structure were adduced to prove this thesis.   I well remember listening to a lecture in which Huxley demolished it.

Less use is made of Scripture now for political purposes than in the days of Gregory the Seventh or even in those of Jefferson Davis.   But attempts to press science into the service of politics are not unknown in our generation, so we must not be surprised that a nation which is nothing if not scientific should have sought and found in what is called the Darwinian Doctrine of Natural Selection a proof of their view that the elimination of the weak by the strong is a principle of universal potency, the method by which progress is attained in the social and political, no less than in the natural sphere.

Their argument has been stated thus: The geological record shows that more highly developed forms have been through countless ages evolved from forms simpler and more rudimentary.   Cryptogamous plants — such as lichens, mosses, ferns — come first, and out of these the phanerogamous were developed. Animal life began with zoophytes and molluscs; serpents and birds followed; then came the mammalia, these culminating in Man. Some species disappeared, and were replaced in the perpetual struggle for existence by others that had proved themselves stronger. Every species fights to maintain itself against the others; there is not room enough for all; the weak disappear, the stronger prevail. So the earlier forms of man himself have succumbed to others superior in strength; and among these latter some races have shown a greater capacity, physical and mental, and have either displaced or exterminated or conquered the weaker, sometimes enslaving them, sometimes absorbing them. When the conquered survive, they receive the impress of the conqueror and are conformed to his more perfect type. Thus the white man has prevailed against the coloured man. Thus the Teuton is prevailing against the Slav and the Celt, and is indeed fitted by his higher gift for intellectual creation, as well as practical organization, to be the Lord of the World, as the lion is lord of the forest and the eagle lord of the air.

As progress in the animal creation is effected by a strife in which the animal organisms possessing most force prevail and endure, so progress in the political world comes through conflicts in which the strongest social organisms, that is, the states best equipped for war, prove themselves able to overcome the weaker. Without war this victory of the best cannot come about. Hence, war is a main cause of progress.

Lest this summary should misrepresent the view I am endeavouring to state — and it is not easy to state it correctly, for there lurks in it some mental confusion — I will cite a few passages from one of its exponents, slightly abridging his words for convenience of quotation.[1] Others have probably stated it better, but all that need be done here is to show how some, at least, of those who hold it have expressed themselves.

" Wherever we look in Nature we find that war is a fundamental law of development. This great verity, which has been recognized in past ages, has been convincingly demonstrated in modern times by Charles Darwin. He proved that nature is ruled by an unceasing struggle for existence, by the right of the stronger, and that this struggle in its apparent cruelty brings about a selection eliminating the weak and the unwholesome."

" The natural law to which all the laws of nature can be reduced is the law of struggle."

" From the first beginning of life, war has been the basis of all healthy development. Struggle is not merely the destructive, but the life-giving principle. The law of the stronger holds good everywhere. Those forms survive which are able to secure for themselves the most favourable conditions of life. The weaker succumb."

Now, let us examine this so-called argument from the biological world and see whether or how far it supports the thesis that the law of progress through strife is a universal law, applicable to human communities as well as to animals and plants.

Several objections present themselves. First. This theory is an attempt to apply what are called Natural Laws to a sphere unlike that of external nature. The facts we study in the external world are wholly different from those we study in human society. There are in that society certain generally observable sequences of phenomena which we popularly call laws of social

1 *Germany and the Next War*, by General von Bernhardi, p. 18.

development: that is to say, individual men and communities of men show certain recurrent tendencies which
may be compared with the recurrent sequences in the
behaviour of inanimate substances and in the animated
creation. But the human or social sequences have not
that uniformity, that generality, that capacity for being
counted or measured, and thereby expressed in precise
and unvarying terms, which belong to things in the
world of external nature. Oxygen and sulphur always
and everywhere behave (so far as we know) in exactly
the same way when the conditions are exactly the same.
Every oak tree and every apple tree, however different
the individuals of the species may be in size, grow in
the same way, and the laws of their growth can be so
stated as to be applicable to all members of the species.
But we cannot do more than conjecture, with more or
less confidence, but never with certainty of prediction,
how any given man or any given community of men will
behave under any given set of conditions.

The human body no doubt consists of tissues, and
the tissues of cells. But each individual in the species
Homo Sapiens Europaeus has, when considered as a
human being, something peculiar to himself which is
not and cannot be completely known or measured. His
action is due to so many complex and hidden causes,
and is therefore so incalculable by any scientific ap-
paratus, he is played upon by so many forces whose
presence and strength no qualitative or quantitative
analysis can determine, that both his thoughts and his
conduct are practically unpredictable. That which we
call a scientific law is therefore totally different in the
social world from what it is in the world of external
nature. Considerations drawn from the latter world
are accordingly, when applied to man, not arguments
but, at best, mere analogies, sometimes suggestive as

indicating lines of inquiry, but never approaching the character of exact science.

Secondly. That which is called the Darwinian principle of Natural Selection is a matter still in controversy among scientific men. A distinguished zoologist, for instance, Dr. Chalmers Mitchell, whose little book entitled *Evolution and the War* may be commended as full of interest and instruction, pronounces the principle to be only a highly probable hypothesis regarding the process by which the evolution of species has taken place, but still no more, as yet, than a hypothesis. The methods by which natural selection takes place are uncertain. Higher and more complex forms do certainly come out of lower and simpler forms; and the adaptability to environment would seem to be an extremely important factor in their development. More than that — so one gathers from the biologists — we are not entitled to assert.

Thirdly. The Struggle for Life in the Darwinian sense is not so much a combat between species as a combat between individuals of the same species, which, like the seeds of plants, dispute the same bit of soil, or, like the carnivorous animals, feed on the same creatures and find there is not enough to go round. In the animal world we find nothing that really resembles the wars of human tribes or states. Tigers or other bellicose animals do not fight either with other tigers or with such other feline tribes as leopards. Individuals may fight in those occasional cases where the possession of the same female is disputed by two males; but groups do not fight each other. Tigers kill antelopes for food; they have no impulse to dominate or to extirpate, but only desire to support their own life. If zoology furnishes any analogy to the contests of nations, it is to be found, not in the clash of Teutonic and Slavonic armies, but where there is an appropriation, by individuals possessing superior industry and skill, of the means of livelihood and opportunities for amassing wealth which trade and civilized finance offer to all alike who will address themselves to the task. Here we see not war, but a competition for means of livelihood.

Fourthly. The supersession of one species by another is certainly not effected, in the external world, by fighting, but apparently by the adaptation to its environment of the species which ultimately survives. Where an oceanic island like Hawaii is overrun by new species of plants whose seeds, or seedlings, are brought from another country, what happens is that some of the new species thus introduced find in the isle an environment of soil and climate which suits them so well that they multiply and crowd out, by their natural growth in the soil, the weaker of the native species established there, till at last a mixed flora results, representing both the old natives and other species from elsewhere. In 1883, when I saw it, Hawaii had thrice been thus overrun. You may see a somewhat similar process where the turf has been cut off a piece of land, leaving it bare for seeds to settle on. Various species appear, some perhaps hardly known before in the neighbourhood; but after some years a few will be found in exclusive possession. Here we have a phenomenon to which there are parallels in the rapid growth and increase of some trees in certain situations which favour them and the consequent displacement of others. But there is nothing like this in human war. And, on the other hand, there is in the animal world no parallel to the fundamental fact that in human warfare it is not the weaker but the stronger part of the population that is drawn away to perish on the battlefield.

Fifthly. We must note in this connection two other important factors in the extension and decline of species. One of them is liability to disease. The other is fecundity. Here an analogy between plants and animals, on the one hand, and the races or sub-races of mankind may no doubt be traced. But there is here no conflict. The causes which make some species more susceptible to maladies than others, or make some more prolific than others, exist everywhere in animated nature. But they exist in the species, or race, being due to something in its peculiar constitution. They have nothing to do with conflict between one species, or one race, and another species or race. That these physical factors have more to do with the numerical strength of a species than has its capacity for fighting becomes so clear when we compare the diffusion of some non-predatory with some predatory species, that it is not worth while to adduce instances. It may be noted, however, that in some of the most advanced races of man the birth-rate is so much lower than it is in the backward races as to threaten the ultimate supremacy of the former.

These considerations, which I have been obliged to state only in outline, seem sufficient to show how hollow is the argument which recommends war as the general law of the universe and a main cause of progress in the human as well as the natural world. It is not an argument at all, but an analogy, and an imperfect one at that. Let me add that the view which regards war as a useful factor in human development had no support from Darwin himself.[1] So far from considering war a cause of progress in general, or of improvement in the population of a particular country, he wrote, in the *Origin of Species*: " In every country in which a

---

1 My friend, Major Leonard Darwin, in a letter which appeared in the Press in 1914, expressly denied that his illustrious father had ever countenanced this application of his theory of Natural Selection. He considered that war tended to the injury of the human species by killing off the best.

large standing army is kept up, the finest young men are taken by conscription or enlisted. They are thus exposed to early death during war, are often tempted into vice, and are prevented from marrying during the prime of life. On the other hand, the shorter and feebler men, with poor constitutions, are left at home, and consequently have a much better chance of marrying."

III

So much for the first set of grounds on which the war theorists rely. Let us turn to the second, that is to say, the argument from history. It is alleged that the record of all that man has done and suffered is largely a record of constant strife — a fact undeniably true — and that thereby the races and nations and states which are now able to do most for the further advance of mankind have prevailed. They have prevailed by war; war, therefore, has been the means, and the necessary means, of that predominance which has enabled them to civilize the best parts of the globe.

Before entering this part of the enquiry, let us see what Progress means. It is a term which covers several quite different things.

There is Material progress, by which I understand an increase in wealth, that is, in the commodities useful to man, which give him health, strength, and longer life, and make his life easier, providing more comfort and more leisure, and thus enabling him to be more physically efficient, and to escape from that pressure of want which hampers the development of his whole nature.

There is Intellectual progress — an increase in knowledge, a greater abundance of ideas, the training to think, and think correctly, the growth in capacity

for dealing with practical problems, the cultivation of
the power to enjoy the exercise of thought and the
pleasures of letters and art.

There is Moral progress, a thing harder to define,
but which includes the development of those emotions
and habits which make for happiness — contentment
and tranquillity of mind, the absence of the more purely
animal and therefore degrading vices (such as intem-
perance and sensuality in its other forms), the control
of the violent passions, good-will and kindliness toward
others — in fact all the things which fall within the
philosophical conception of a life guided by right reason. People have different ideas of what constitutes
happiness and virtue, but these things are at any rate
included in every such conception.

A further preliminary question arises. Is human
progress to be estimated as respects the point to which
it raises the few who have high mental gifts and the
opportunity of obtaining an education fitting them for
intellectual enjoyment and intellectual vocations, or is
it to be measured by the amount of its extension to and
diffusion through each nation, meaning the nation as a
whole — the average man as well as the superior
spirits? You may sacrifice either the many to the few
— as was done by slavery — or the few to the many,
or the advance may be general and proportionate in all
classes.

Again, when we think of Progress, are we to think
of the world as a whole, or only of the stronger and
more capable races and states? If the stronger rise
upon the prostrate bodies of the weaker, is this clear
gain to the world, because the stronger will ultimately
do more for the world, or is the loss and suffering of
the weaker to be brought into the account? I do not
attempt to discuss these questions. It is enough to

note them as fit to be remembered; for perhaps all three kinds of progress ought to be differently judged if a few leading nations only are to be regarded, or if we are to think of all mankind.

Now let us address ourselves to history. Does history show that progress has come more through and by war or through and by peace? It would be tedious to pursue an examination of the question all down the annals of mankind from the days when authentic records begin; but we may take a few of those salient instances to which the advocates of the war doctrine and those of the peace doctrine would appeal as sustaining their respective theses. Let us divide these instances into four classes, as follows:

(1) Instances cited to show that War promotes Progress.

(2) Instances cited to show that Peace has failed to promote Progress.

(3) Instances cited to show that War has failed to promote Progress.

(4) Instances cited to show that Peace promotes Progress.

I begin with the cases in which war is alleged to have been the cause of progress.

It is undeniable that war has often been accompanied by an advance in civilization. If we were to look for progress only in times of peace there would have been little progress to discover, for mankind has lived in a state of practically continuous warfare. The Egyptian and Assyrian monarchs were always fighting. The Book of Samuel speaks of spring as the time when kings go forth to battle, much as we should speak of autumn as the time when men go forth to shoot deer. Πόλεμος φύσει ὑπάρχει πρὸς ἁπάσας τὰς πόλεις,[1] said Plato.

---

[1] War is the natural relation of states to one another.

Things have not greatly improved since those distant days, though latterly men have become accustomed to think of peace as the normal, war as the abnormal or exceptional, relation of states to one another. In the ancient world, as late as the days of Roman conquest, a state of peace was the rare exception among civilized states as well as barbarous tribes. But Carthage, like her Phoenician mother-city, went on building up a mighty commerce till Rome smote her down, and the Hellenic people, in its many warring cities, went on producing noble poems and profound philosophical speculations, and rearing majestic temples and adorning them with incomparable works of sculpture, in the intervals of their fighting with their neighbours of the same and other races. The case of the Greeks proves that War and Progress are compatible. Whoever visits Sicily and the coasts of the Aegean cannot but be struck by the thought that it was in the midst of warfare that the majestic buildings of these regions were erected at enormous cost.

The case of Rome is still more often dwelt upon. Her material greatness was due to the conquests which made her mistress of the world. She also achieved intellectual greatness in her poets and orators and jurists, and by her literature and her laws contributed immensely to the progress of mankind. How far are these achievements to be credited to that long course of conquest?

The Temple of Janus had stood open as a sign of war for two hundred years, when it was closed by Augustus in 29 B.C. to indicate the general peace he had established. The spirit of the Roman people was sustained at a high level by military triumphs, as discipline and the capacity for organization and united national action were also engendered and sustained.

But it is to be noted that, although the Romans had shown great political intelligence in creating and working their curiously complex constitution, their literary production attained no high level until Hellenic influences had worked upon it.   To these influences, more than to any material causes, its excellence is due.   Nor did the creative epoch last long.   War continued; but production declined both in letters and in art after the days of the great warrior Trajan, though there was more fighting than ever.   The waning strength of the Empire, as well as the economic decay of Italy, has been justly attributed in large measure to the exhaustion by warfare of the old Italian stock.

In the thirteenth, fourteenth, and fifteenth centuries, when civilization had greatly advanced in southern and western Europe, the phenomena of ancient Greece were repeated.   Incessant wars between the cities of Italy did not prevent the growth of a brilliant literature and an even more brilliant art.   It is, however, to be noted that, while the fighting was universal, the literature was confined to comparatively few centres, and there were places like the Neapolitan South, in which high artistic talent was rare.   There is nothing in Italian history to show any causal connection between intellectual activity and the practice of war.   The same may be said of France.   The best work in literature and art was done in a time of comparative tranquillity under Louis XIV., not in the more troubled days of the Hundred Years' War with England and of the religious wars of the sixteenth century.

The capital instance of the association of war with the growth and greatness of a state is found in Prussia. One may say that her history is the source of the whole thesis and the basis of the whole argument.   It is a case of what, in the days when the students of my

generation were learning logic at the University of
Oxford, we used to call the " induction from a single
instance." Prussia, then a small state, began her up-
ward march under the warlike and successful prince
whom her people call the Great Elector. Her next
long step to greatness was taken by Frederick II., again
by a course of successful warfare, though doubtless also
by means of a highly organized, and, for those days,
very efficient administration. Voltaire said of Frederick's Prussia that its trade was war. The close of
the Napoleonic wars further enlarged her territory.
Three successful wars — those of 1864, 1866, and
1870–71 — made her the nucleus of a united German
nation and the leading military power of the Old
World.

Ever since those victories her industrial production,
her commerce, and her wealth have rapidly increased,
while at the same time scientific research has been prosecuted with the greatest vigour and on a scale unprece-
dentedly large. These things were no doubt achieved
during a peace of forty-three years. But it was what
one may call a belligerent peace, full of thoughts of
war and preparations for war. There is no denying
that the national spirit has been carried to a high point
of pride, energy, and self-confidence, which have stimulated effort in all directions and secured extraordinary
efficiency in civil as well as in military administration.
Here, then, is an instance in which a state has grown
by war and a people has been energized by war.

But before drawing any conclusions from this soli-
tary instance three questions must be asked:

Will the present conflict be attended by such a success as to lead the Prussian people to approve the policy
which this war spirit has inspired?

Even supposing that the nation is not defeated and

humbled in the struggle, may not its material prosperity be thrown back and its internal tranquillity impaired?

May not the national character turn out to have suffered a declension which it will take long to cure?

Results cannot be judged at the moment. What people was ever prouder of its world-dominion than the Romans at the time of Augustus? Yet the seeds of decline were already sown. Within a century, men like Tacitus had begun to note the signs of a slowly approaching dissolution. and within two centuries more the dissolution was at hand. To this it may be added that the advance of any single state by violent methods may involve greater harm to the world than the benefits which that state expects to gain for itself, or than those which it proposes to confer upon its neighbours by imposing its civilization upon them.

I pass to another set of cases, those in which it is argued that the absence of war has meant the absence of progress. Such cases are rare, because so few countries have enjoyed, or had the chance of suffering from, periods of long peace. Two, however, may be referred to. One is supplied by the Spanish dominions in America from the middle of the sixteenth till the beginning of the nineteenth century, when they threw off the yoke of the mother-country. These vast countries, stretching from California to Patagonia, lay lapped in a peace disturbed only by the occasional raids of Dutch or British sea-rovers, and by skirmishes, rarely severe, with native Indian tribes. The Spanish colonies certainly did stagnate, and made no sensible advance either materially or intellectually. But peace was not the cause of their stagnation. It may be easily explained by the facts that they were ruled by a government at once autocratic and incapable, and that they lived so far from the European world of ideas as to be hardly affected by its vivifying influences.   Such causes were amply sufficient to arrest progress.

The other case, often cited, is that of China.   She is supposed to have become flaccid, feeble, immovably conservative, because her people, long unaccustomed to war, have contracted a pacific temper.   In this statement there is some exaggeration, for there has always been a good deal of fighting on the outskirts of the Chinese Empire; and in the Tae Ping insurrection forty years ago millions of men are said to have been killed.   It must also be remembered that in Art, at least — one of the activities in which the Chinese hold a leading place — there have been frequent changes and some brilliant revivals during the centuries of peace.   China reached in comparatively early times a civilization very remarkable on its moral and intellectual as well as on its material side.   That her subsequent progress was slow, sometimes hardly discernible, is mainly attributable to her complete isolation, with no nation near her from which she had anything to learn, because the tribes to the southwest and west — tribes constantly occupied in war — were far inferior to her.   Lucky has it been for the rest of the world that her three hundred and fifty millions, belonging to a race both physically strong and capable of discipline, have been of a pacific temper, valuing trade and industry, artistic creation and skill in literary composition, as objects worthier of man than martial prowess.

Whoever travels among the Chinese sees that, peaceful as they are, they are anything but a decadent or exhausted race.   Nor is it idle to remark that the Japanese, a really military people, had during many centuries made no more progress than their Chinese teachers, and for the same reason: viz. that they had remained, down to our own time, cut off, and that by their own wish, from all the stimulating influences which the white races were exerting upon one another.

Next, let us take the cases which show that there have been in many countries long periods of incessant war with no corresponding progress in the things that make civilization. I will not speak of peoples tribally organized, among the more advanced of which may be placed the Albanians and the Pathans and the Turkomans, while among the more backward were the North American Indians and the Zulus. But one may cite the case of the civilized regions of Asia under the successors of Alexander, when civilized peoples, distracted by incessant strife, did comparatively little for the progress of arts or letters or government, from the death of the great conqueror till they were united under the dominion of Rome and received from her a time of almost unbroken tranquillity.

The Thirty Years' War is an example of long-continued fighting, which, far from bringing progress in its train, inflicted injuries on Germany from which she did not recover for nearly two centuries. Nearer our times, there has been more fighting in South and Central America, since the Wars of Independence, than in any other civilized countries. Yet can any one say that anything has been gained by the unending civil wars and revolutions, or those scarcely less frequent conflicts between the several republics, like that terrible one thirty years ago in which Peru was overcome by Chile? Or look at Mexico. Except during the years when the stern dictatorship of Porfirio Diaz kept order and equipped the country with roads and railways, her people have made no perceptible advance, and stand hardly higher to-day than when they were left to work

out their own salvation a hundred years ago.   Social
and economic conditions have doubtless been against
her.   All that need be remembered is that warfare has
not bettered those conditions, or improved the national
character.

Last of all we come to cases in which periods of
peace have been attended by an increase in national
prosperity and by intellectual development.   These
periods have been few and generally short, for (as
already observed) war has been everywhere the rule
and peace the exception.   Nevertheless, one may point
to instances like that of the comparative order and re-
pose which England enjoyed after the Wars of the
Roses.   There were some foreign wars under the
Tudors; there were brilliant achievements and adven-
tures on the seas.   There were some few internal re-
volts under Elizabeth.   But the great bulk of the nation was left free to prosper by agriculture and trade
and to produce great writers.   It was the century of
More and Bacon and Harvey, of Sidney and Spencer
and Shakespeare.   Two similar instances are furnished
by the rapid progress of Scotland after the Revolution
of 1688–89 gave her internal peace, and the similar
progress of Norway from 1814 till our own days.
The annals of Switzerland since 1815 and those of
Belgium since her creation in 1832 have shown that a
peace maintained during two generations is compatible,
not only with the rapid growth of industrial prosperity,
but also with the preservation of a courageous and
patriotic spirit, ready to face the dangers of war.

IV

If this hasty historical survey has, as I frankly admit,
given us few positive and definite results, the reason
is plain.   Human progress is affected by so many con-

ditions besides the presence or absence of fighting, that
it is impossible in any given case to pronounce that it
has been chiefly due either to war or to peace. Two
conclusions, however, we may claim to have reached,
though they are rather negative than positive. One is
that war does not necessarily arrest progress. Peoples may advance in thought, literature, and art while
they are fighting. The other is that war cannot be
shown to have been a cause of progress in anything
except the wealth or material power of a state which
extends its dominions by conquest or fills its coffers by
tribute extorted from the vanquished.

In those cases, however, where the victorious state
has gained materially, there are two other things to be
considered. One is the possible loss to the conqueror
of the good-will of other nations who may reprobate
its methods or fear its aggressive tendencies. Another
is the political injury it may suffer by sacrificing, as usually happens with military states, its domestic freedom
to its achievements in war, or the moral injury which
the predominance of warlike ideals is apt to bring to
national character. And if we extend our view to take
in the general gain or loss to world-progress, the benefits reaped by the victorious state may be more than
counterbalanced by the harm inflicted on the vanquished. When the Macedonian kings destroyed the
freedom of Greece, did not mankind lose far more
than Macedon gained?

The weakness of the argument which recommends
and justifies war by the suggestion that it is by war that
the foremost races and states have established their
position may be very briefly stated. War has been
practically universal. All the races and states have
fought, some better, some worse. The best fighters
have not always succeeded, for they may have been

fewer in number. There is no necessary connection
between fighting quality and intellectual quality. True
it is that some of the intellectually gifted peoples have
also been warlike peoples. The Greeks were; so are
the French and Germans. But the Turks, who are
good fighters, are good for nothing else; and the dull
Spartans fought better, on land at least, than the
bright Athenians. Where the gift for fighting goes
with the gift for thought, the success achieved by the
intellectual race in war is not a result but a symptom,
an indication or evidence of an exceptional natural
force. Those races and states that are now in the
front rank of civilization have shown their capacity in
many other fields besides that of war, and at other
times than when they were fighting. All that can safely
be said to be proved by history is that a race which
cannot fight or will not fight when a proper occasion
arises, as, for instance, when it has to vindicate its independence, is likely to go down, and be subjected or
absorbed. Yet the fact that a state is subjected or
absorbed does not prove its inferiority. There is no
poetical justice in history. The highly gifted race
may be small, like Israel, or too much divided to maintain itself against heavy odds, like the Hellenes of
antiquity. From 1490 to 1560 Italy was the prey of
foreign invaders; but she was doing more for human
progress in art and letters than all the other European
nations put together.

So far, then, our inquiry has shown two things.
One is the worthlessness of the biological analogy —
for it is only an analogy — between animated nature
and human society, based upon what is called the
Struggle for Life and the Survival of the Fittest. The
other is the weakness of the arguments drawn from
history to prove war necessary to progress.

V

Let us now, in conclusion, try to approach the question in another way. Let us ask what are the consequences which seem naturally to flow from the devotion to war of a nation's gifts and powers, whether physical or intellectual. Reverting to the distinction already drawn between Material, Intellectual, and Moral progress, let us see what are the consequences to be expected in each of these spheres from that process of killing an enemy and capturing or destroying his property which we call War, and how far they will make for the general progress of mankind.

Materially regarded, War is Destruction. It is the destruction of those who are killed, and the reduction, by maiming or disease, of the physical working power of the combatants who survive. It is thus a diminution of the wealth-producing capacity of the combatant nations, whether they be victors or vanquished. It means also the destruction of articles of value, such as crops, railways, bridges, and other buildings, and the contents of buildings, including works of art and libraries. It is an interruption of international trade as well as of production, and therefore a cutting-off, for the time being, of that other source of gain which consists in an exchange of commodities produced better or more cheaply in one country than they can be in another. It involves a further lessening of wealth by the withdrawal from their productive activities of a large number of workers, not only during the actual fighting, but during the time spent in being trained to fight. All these results mean waste of resources and the impoverishment of a nation, with a corresponding shock to its credit.

Against these losses there may be set, in the case of

a conquering country, what it acquires by seizure of property, annexation of territory, levying of contributions and of indemnities, although these forcibly gotten gains do not always prosper. There may also be new openings to foreign trade, and victory may evoke an enterprising spirit which will push that trade with new vigour. But such possible indirect benefits are usually far outweighed by the direct loss.

Another loss is also to be considered in estimating the effects of war on a nation. There is not only the diminution of the population by death in battle, but also the reduced vigour and efficiency of the next generation. Those who are killed are presumably the strongest and healthiest men, for it is these who are the first to be drafted into the fighting forces; and it is the best regiments that suffer most, because they are selected for the most critical and perilous enterprises. Thus, that part of the nation which is best fitted to have a vigorous progeny perishes, and the births of children during, and long after, the war will be chiefly from a male parenthood of a quality below that of the average as it stood before the war. The physique of the French people is said to have suffered palpably from the tremendous drain of the strongest men into the armies of the Revolution and of Napoleon.

In the sphere of intellectual life, the obvious effect of war is to turn the thoughts of a large part of the nation toward military and naval topics. Inventors busy themselves with those physical and chemical researches which promise results profitable for war. Such researches may incidentally lead to discoveries of value in other fields, just as the practice of military surgery in the field may advance surgical science in general. But the main effect must be to distract from pure science, and from the applications of science to industry, minds that might have done better work for the world in those fields of activity. In general, the thought of a people that delights in war will be occupied with material considerations; and while the things of the body will be prized, the things of the mind will be disparaged, save in so far as they make for military success. A fighting caste will be formed, imposing its peculiar ideals on the people; the standards of value will become more and more practical, and the interest in pure truth and in thought and art for their own sake may decline.

These are conditions not favourable to progress in the higher forms of literary or scientific work. Against them is to be set that stimulus which a great war is held to give to the whole life of a people. When it rouses them to the maximum of effort, and gives them the strongest consciousness of national unity, it may also — so we hear it argued — invigorate them for intellectual creation. It would be rash to deny this possibility, but no one seems to have succeeded in tracing any causal relation between war and the production of great work in art and letters. They have often coincided, but each has often appeared without the other.

Note also how misleading it may be to apply the doctrine of Natural Selection to the phenomena of human society, even so far as it may safely be applied in zoology. Within a nation it is not strength alone, whether physical or intellectual, that brings success. The power of self-control, the talent of co-operating with others, the capacity for inspiring confidence, are no less important both in securing influence for the possessor of these gifts and in contributing to the unity and energy of a nation. Similarly a nation's vitality consists not only in the physical and mental powers of its members, but also in their moral qualities, their patriotism, their capacity for devotion and self-sacrifice, their good faith and uprightness, their respect for law as law — qualities to which the Romans, for instance, were wont to ascribe their greatness. Natural Selection assumes the rule of Force. But Force and Law are opposed: Force Worship is the negation of Right expressed in Law, and those who have been taught to contemn Right and to put their trust in Force may not only injure themselves, but raise up fears and hatreds against them in their neighbour nations.

As respects the ethical side of life, soldiering and the preparation for soldiering produce a type of character marked by discipline and the habit of obedience. The Spartans were in the ancient world the example of a people who excelled in these qualities, uniting to them, however, an equally marked insensibility to the charms of poetry and art. They produced no literature, and seemed to value none except martial songs. Discipline has its worth, but it may imply some loss of individuality; obedience is useful, but (except with the highly intelligent) it involves some loss of initiative. If it increases physical courage, it may depress that moral courage which recognizes allegiance to Right rather than to the Might of the State. War gives opportunities for the display, by those serving in the field, of some exalted virtues, such as courage, self-sacrifice, devotion to the common cause. So, likewise, does religious persecution, but we do not therefore persecute. Tennyson, writing his *Maud* at the beginning of the Crimean War, seems to have expected these virtues to be evoked by that war, to pervade the whole people, and to effect a moral regeneration of Britain. Did that happen? And if it happened, did it endure? Did it happen in other countries where it was expected, as, for instance, in the United States after the Civil War? Is such regeneration a natural fruit of war?

The courage and the patriotism of those who fight are splendid, but we have to think of the nation as a whole, non-combatants as well as combatants. May not much depend on the causes which have brought about an appeal to arms and the motives which inspire the combatants? A war of oppression, stimulated by national pride and ambition, may have a different moral effect from one that is undertaken to repel a wanton attack, to defend an innocent neutral state, to save peaceful peoples from a danger to their liberties, and protect the whole world from a menace to the sacred principles of justice and humanity.

Believing the war we are now waging to be such a war, we cannot but hope that the unspeakable sufferings and sorrows it has brought to nearly every home in Britain may be largely compensated by a purifying of the heart, an increased spirit of self-sacrifice, and a raising of our national and personal ideals.

On a review of the whole matter, it will appear that war, since it is destruction, does not increase, but reduces, national wealth, and therefore cannot be a direct cause of material progress. As it exalts physical strength and the principle of Force as against the mind and the love of truth and the pleasures of thought and knowledge, war, except so far as the particular department of military science is concerned, cannot be deemed a cause of intellectual progress. As it depresses the individual and exalts the State, the thing we call Militarism places the conception of Might above that of Right, and creates a type of character in which the harsher, and what one may call the heathen, virtues are exalted above those which the Gospel has taught and

through which the moral elevation of the world has
been secured.

What, then, are the causes to which the progress of
mankind is due? It has come partly, no doubt, if not
of strife, yet at any rate in the course of competition.
But the chief cause is the exercise of creative thought in
the sphere of ideas, in scientific discovery, in inventions.
Now Thought, as we have seen, is more often hindered
than helped by war. It is the races that know how to
think, not the far more numerous races that excel in
fighting rather than in thinking, that have led the world.
Thought, in the form of invention and scientific inquiry,
has given us those improvements in the arts of life and
in the knowledge of nature by which material progress
and comfort have been obtained. Thought has produced literature, philosophy, art, and (when intensified
by emotion) religion — the chief things that make life
worth living. Now, the thought of any people is most
active when it is brought into contact with the thought
of another, because each is apt to lose its variety and
freedom to play when it has worked too long upon
familiar lines and flowed too long in the channels it has
deepened. Hence, Isolation retards progress, while
Intercourse quickens it.

The great creative epochs have been those in which
one people of natural vigour received an intellectual
impulse from the ideas of another, as happened when
Greek culture began to penetrate Italy, and, thirteen
centuries later, when the literature of the ancients began
to work on the nations of the mediaeval world.

Such contact, with the process of learning which
follows from it, may happen in or through war, but it
happens far oftener in peace; and it is in peace that
men have the time and the taste to profit fully by it.
A study of history will show that we may, with an easy

conscience, dismiss the doctrine of Treitschke — that war is a health-giving tonic which Providence must be expected constantly to offer to the human race for its own good. The spirit which every class in the community has shown, since August 1914, in volunteering to fight and in fighting has shown that a long peace does not impair the courage and the valour of a people.[1] Apart altogether from the hopes we entertain for the victory in this war of a cause which we believe to be just, we may desire in the interests of all mankind that its issue should discredit by defeat a theory which is noxious as well as baseless. The future progress of mankind is to be sought, not through the strifes and hatreds of the nations, but rather by their friendly co-operation in the healing and enlightening works of peace, and in the growth of a spirit of friendship and mutual confidence which may remove the causes of war.

1 The same may now (1918) be said of the people of the United States.

CHAPTER V

[THIS and the following chapter contain two Annual Presidential addresses delivered in 1915 and 1916 to the British Academy for the promotion of historical, philological, and philosophical studies, with the omission of those parts which related to the work done by the Academy itself during the two years preceding, viz. the undertakings it directs, the papers read before it, and the lectures delivered on the foundations it administers, together with the obituary notices of Fellows deceased. These general portions of the two addresses were first published in 1916 by the desire of the Council of the British Academy. They treat of certain aspects of the present war, and of war in general, which have an interest for historians and for students of human nature.

References to current political issues, national or international, are necessarily absent, because those topics lie outside the scope of the Academy's functions, and are never discussed at its meetings.]

PRESIDENTIAL ADDRESS DELIVERED TO THE BRITISH ACADEMY, JUNE 30, 1915

In the scantiness of a record of work done in the fields which the Academy cultivates, it might be expected that I should offer to you some remarks on the war itself, the causes that produced it, the antagonisms, deeper than most people supposed, which it has revealed, and the changes it is likely to involve. But many of you will have felt, and all will admit, the dangers that surround any one who, influenced by strong emotions and possessing imperfect knowledge, should now commit to print his judgment of the events of the last eleven months.   Every one among us must sometimes have had cause to regret, when reading them years afterwards, words which he wrote in the heat of the moment.   Time modifies our judgments as it cools our passions.   Neither the friendships nor the enmities of nations are exempt from change.   You remember how Ajax, in the drama of Sophocles, says that he has learnt

$$\ddot{o} \ \tau' \ \dot{\epsilon}\chi\theta\rho\dot{o}s \ \dot{\eta}\mu\hat{\iota}\nu \ \dot{\epsilon}s \ \tau\sigma\sigma\dot{o}\nu\delta' \ \dot{\epsilon}\chi\theta\alpha\rho\tau\dot{\epsilon}os$$
$$\dot{\omega}s \ \kappa\alpha\dot{\iota} \ \phi\iota\lambda\dot{\eta}\sigma\omega\nu \ \alpha\dot{\upsilon}\theta\iota s\cdot$$

I am, however, in any case debarred by the rules and practice of the Academy from entering the field of current politics.   It is better that nothing should be said to-day in an address to the Academy which any one of its members, to whatever country he may belong, would feel pain in reading ten or twenty years hence. Newspapers and pamphlets will convey to posterity sufficiently, and even more than sufficiently, the notions and fancies and passions of the moment.

What we may do, not without profit, is to note and to set down in a spirit of detachment the impressions made upon us by the events which our eyes see and watch as they pass into history.   Many a pen will for centuries to come be occupied by the events of this year, and endless controversies will arise over them.   It is well that whoever has gained from his studies something of an historical sense should in the spirit proper to an historian place on record from month to month the impressions he receives.   The record will be almost as useful if the impressions should turn out to be erroneous as if they should be confirmed by subsequent

events, because what the future historian will desire to
know is not only what happened but what people believed and thought at the time it was happening.   That
which is omitted has also its value.   Fifty years hence
men will be struck by the significance of things whose
significance was not perceived by contemporary observers, and will seek to know why those observers failed
to see or comprehend facts which will then stand out in
bold relief.

So let me now try to enumerate briefly what are the
facts of the present situation by which we are chiefly
impressed — facts that make it novel as well as terrible.

The first fact is the immense width and range of the
war.   Thucydides observed that men always thought
the war they were then engaged in the greatest that had
ever befallen.   But here we have facts which show how
much the present conflict does transcend any seen in
previous ages.   This might have been foretold twenty
years ago, assuming that Russia, Germany, and Britain
were involved, seeing how vast are the possessions and
claims and ambitions of all three States.   Yet the
reality goes far beyond every forecast.   All the six
great European Powers and four lesser Powers are
involved.[1]   So is the whole extra-European Old
World, except China and Persia and the possessions of
Holland and Portugal.   In the New World it is only
the Dominions and Colonies of Britain that are as
yet affected — a noteworthy illustration of the severance of the Western hemisphere from the broils of the
Eastern.

Secondly.   There is the prodigious influence of the

---

[1] Since this was written three other European Powers have entered the war,
the Portuguese colonies have also become involved, and not only the United
States, with its population exceeding one hundred millions, but Brazil and
Cuba also have followed.

war upon neutral nations. This also might have been foreseen as a result of the development of world commerce and the interlockings of world finance. But here too, the actual results are transcending expectation.

Thirdly. The changes in the methods and character of war have been far more extensive than in any previous period. It took much more than two centuries from the invention of gunpowder for musketry and artillery to supersede completely archery and defensive armour. The long pike, after having been used for some twenty-five centuries at least, was still in use as late as the Irish Rebellion of 1798, and to a slight extent in the abortive rising of 1848. War, however, is now a totally different thing from what it was in the campaign of 1870–71, or even in the war between Russia and Japan of 1904. Chemistry has changed everything by increasing the range and the power of missiles, while electricity, without the wire, supplies new means of communication not only along battle lines, but across hostile territory. So the application of photography to war has enabled the position of enemy entrenchments or forces to be so located that artillery can now play effectively upon spots which those who direct the fire cannot see. Warfare in the air and warfare under the sea were heretofore mere dreams.

Fourthly. The cost of war is greater in proportion to the size of armies, immensely larger as these armies are, than it ever was before. The ten belligerent European Powers are estimated to be spending now more than ten millions sterling a day.[1] At this rate their total expenditure for twelve months could not be less than 4000 millions, and may be much more. But some competent economists put it at 5000 millions, figures which are hardly more realizable by us than are

[1] This sum was subsequently much exceeded.

those which express the distances of the fixed stars.

Fifthly. In each nation the whole body of the people is more fully and more hotly interested in, and united by, this war than by any it ever waged before. During the eighteenth century it was in most countries only the monarch and the ruling class that knew or cared what was happening. The great European conflict that began in 1793 brought a change. But this war is far more intensely national, in the sense that it has roused the animosities of the whole of each people from top to bottom, than any preceding conflict, and it is everywhere waged with a sterner purpose. In this respect we are reminded of the citizen wars of the small city-states of ancient Greece and Italy, and of the Italian Middle Ages.

Sixthly. Some grave moral issues have been raised more sharply than before. Is a state above morality? Does the plea of military necessity (of which the State itself is apparently to be the judge) entitle it to disregard the rights of other states? (Cf. Thucydides v. 84–113, the case of Melos.)

Seventhly. The predictions that the vast interests involved, the increasing strength of defence as opposed to attack, and the growth of a general pacific sentiment, would avert strife have all proved fallacious. The wisdom of the wise, where is it now? Many supposed that the great financiers would be able to avert hostilities, and would think it their interest to do so. Some twelve years ago Jean de Bloch, in a book that made a great impression at the time, argued that the growing difficulties of conducting military operations on a vast scale might not only make war a longer and far more costly business than ever before, but even prove an effective deterrent. More recently an accomplished and persuasive English writer has shown how much more a nation has to lose by war than it can possibly gain even if victory crown its arms. Others have thought that a sense of solidarity among the workers in each industrial country would be strong enough to restrain their governments from any but a purely defensive war. Others, again, have declared that democracies are essentially peaceful, because the mass of the people pay in their blood, other classes merely in their wealth. I do not say that these arguments are unsound, but the forces they rely upon have not proved strong enough for the occasion. For practical purposes the wisdom of the wise has been brought to naught, because the rulers of the nations have been guided by other motives than those of pure reason.

These observations relate to the palpable facts we have witnessed. Let us turn now to some of the reflections which the facts suggest. It is not easy to express these with that cold detachment at which the historian is bound to aim; but the effort must be made.

On that reflection which rose first to our minds when the war began, and which continues to be the sombre background to every aspect it presents — upon this I will not pause. After more than forty centuries of civilization and nineteen centuries of Christianity, mankind — in this case at least three-fourths of mankind — is settling its disputes in the same way as mankind did in the Stone Age. The weapons are more various and more destructive. They are the latest product of highly developed science. But the spirit and the result are the same.

There has never been a time in which communications were so easy, and the means for discovering and circulating information so abundant. Yet how little is now certainly known as to the real causes which have brought about the war. The beliefs current among

different peoples are altogether different, not to say con-
tradictory. Some are almost demonstrably false.
Even in some neutral nations such as Holland, Switzerland, and Spain, opinion is sharply divided not merely
about the rights but also about the facts. The whole
German people seem to hold just as implicitly that this
is for them a defensive war as the French hold the
opposite; and however clear the main points may appear to us in Britain, there are others which may remain
obscure for many years to come.

How few are the persons in every state in whose
hands lie the issues of war and peace! In some of the
now belligerent countries the final and vital decisions
were taken by four or five persons only, in others by six
or seven only. Even in Britain decision rested practically with less than twenty-five, for though some few
persons outside the Cabinet took a part, not all within
the Cabinet are to be reckoned as effective factors. It
is of course true that popular sentiment has to be considered, even in states more or less despotically governed. Against a strong and definite sentiment of the
masses the ruling few would not venture to act. But
the masses are virtually led by a few, and their opinion
is formed, particularly at a crisis, by the authority and
the appeals of those few whom they have been accustomed to trust or to obey. And after all, the vital
decision at the vital moment remains with the few. If
they had decided otherwise than they did, the thing
would not have happened. Something like it might
have happened later, but the war would not have come
then and so.

How rapidly do vast events move, how quickly are
vast decisions taken! In the twelve fatal days from
July 23 to August 4 there was no time for reflection.
Telegrams between seven capitals flew hither and

thither like swift arrows crossing one another, and it would have needed a mind of more than human amplitude and energy to grasp and correlate all the issues involved and to foresee the results that would follow the various lines of action possible in a game so complicated.   Even the intellect of a Caesar or a Bonaparte would have been unequal to the task.   Here the telegraph has worked for evil.   Had the communications passed by written dispatches, as they would have done eighty years ago, it is probable that war might have been avoided.

Sometimes one feels as if modern states were growing too huge for the men to whom their fortunes are committed.   Mankind increases in volume, and in accumulated knowledge, and in a comprehension of the forces of nature; but the intellects of individual men do not grow.   The power of grasping and judging in their entirety the far greater mass of facts to be dealt with, the far more abundant resources at command, the far vaster issues involving the weal or woe of masses of men — this power fails to follow.   The disproportion between the individual ruling men with their personal prejudices and proclivities, their selfish interests and their vanities, and the immeasurable consequences which follow their individual volitions, becomes more striking and more tragic.   As the stage expands, the figures shrink.   There were some advantages in the small city-states of antiquity.   A single city might decline or perish, but the nation remained; and another city blossomed forth to replace that which had withered away.   But now enormous nations are concentrated under one government and its disasters affect the whole.   A great modern state is like a gigantic vessel built without any water-tight compartments, which, if it be unskilfully steered, may perish when it strikes a single rock.

How ignorant modern peoples, with all the abundant means of information at their disposal, may nevertheless remain of one another's character and purposes! Each of the nations now at war has evidently had a false notion of its adversaries and has been thereby misled.   It has not known their inner thoughts, it has misread their policy.   It was said in the days of the American Civil War that the misconception by the Southern States of the Northern States, and their belief that the North cared for nothing but the dollar, was the real cause why their differences were not peaceably settled, and yet they were both members of the same Republic and spoke the same language.   European nations cannot be expected to have quite so intimate a knowledge each of the other, yet both their commercial intercourse and the activity of the Press and the immensely increased volume of private travel might have been expected to enable them better to gauge and judge one another's minds.

Historians as far back as Thucydides have made upon the behaviour of nations in war time many general observations, which have been brought out in stronger light by what passes from day to day before us.   A few of these I will mention to suggest how we may turn to account the illustrations which Europe now furnishes.

When danger threatens a nation its habits change. Defence becomes the supreme need.   In place of the ordinary machinery of government there starts up a dictatorship like that of early Rome, when twenty-four lictors surrounded the magistrate and the tribunician veto, with the right of appeal, sank away.   The plea of public interest overrides everything.   The suspension of constitutional guarantees is acquiesced in, and acts of arbitrary power, even if violent, are welcomed because taken as signs of strength in the ruler.   Even the withholding of information is submitted to. The voice of criticism is silenced. *Cedit toga armis.* The soldier comes to the front, speaks with an authority greater than that of the civilian statesman, is permitted to do whatever he declares to be necessary for the nation's safety. So long as that is secured, everything else is pardoned, and success gives enormous prestige.

Whoever watches these things must see how dangerous to freedom is war, except in those communities where long tradition has rooted constitutional habit very deep. In old Greece seditions opened the way to the Tyrant. Napoleon supposed that the Duke of Wellington would, after Waterloo, have made himself master of England. So might a victor of another quality have done who had achieved such a triumph as Wellington's, had not an ancient monarchy and Parliament stood in his way. War is the bane of democracies. If it be civil war, he who restores peace is acclaimed like Augustus. Even a Louis Napoleon may be welcome when he promises security for property. If it be foreign war, the man of the sword on horseback towers over the man on foot who can only talk and administer.

So those psychological phenomena which former observers have noticed when a country is swept by war or revolution, have become vividly real to Europe now. The same passion seizes on every one simultaneously and grows hotter in each by the sense that others share it. It is said that when sheep, feeding unherded on a mountain, see the approach of a danger they all huddle together, the rams on the outside facing the foe. The flock becomes one, with one mind, one fear, one rage of fear. So in times of danger a human community feels and acts like one man. The nation realizes itself so vividly that it becomes a law to itself and recks little of the opinion of others.   The man is lost in the crowd, and the crowd feels rather than thinks.   Passion intensified supersedes the ordinary exercise not only of individual will but even of individual reason.   Fear and anger breed suspicion and credulity.   Every one is ready to believe the worst of whoever is suspected. What is called the power of suggestion rises to such a height that to denounce a man is virtually to condemn him.   Lavoisier is sentenced to be guillotined; he pleads that he is a harmless chemist, but is told that the Republic does not need chemists.   After the death of Julius Caesar, Cinna, the poet, is seized, and when he protests that he is not Cinna the conspirator, is nevertheless killed for his name, the bystander (in Shakespeare) adding, " Kill him for his bad verses."   A foreign name is taken to be evidence that its bearer is a spy.   Grotesquely absurd charges find credence. There is no tolerance for difference of opinion, and to advance arguments against the reigning sentiment is treason.   Any tribute to the character or even to the intellectual gifts of an enemy is resented.   Sentiments of humanity towards him are disapproved, unless the precaution is taken of expressing these in the exact words of Holy Scripture.   The rising flame of hatred involves not merely the government and armies of the enemy, but even the innocent citizens of the hostile country.   These well-known phenomena are all more or less visible in Europe to-day, though in our own country the coolness of our temperament and the fact that no invader has trodden our soil have been presenting them in a comparatively mild type.

The intensification of emotions includes those of a religious kind, and these not always in their purest form.   In most countries it is only the most enlightened minds that can refrain from claiming the Deity as their peculiar protector and taking every victory as a mark of His special favour. Modern man seems at such moments to have reverted to those primitive ages when each tribe fought for its own god and expected its own god to fight for it, as Moab called on Chemosh and Tyre on Melkarth. True it is that a nation now usually argues that Divine protection will be extended to it because its cause is just. But as this is announced by every nation alike, the result is much the same now as it was in the days of Chemosh and Melkarth. Oddly enough, the people in whom fanaticism used to be strongest are now responding more feebly than ever before to the appeal of the *Jihád*. Is it because the Turkish Musulmans have infidel Powers for allies as well as for enemies, or because the men who now rule Turkey are known to fear God as little as they regard man, that this war seems to them less holy than those of the centuries in which their conquests were won?

Upon other symptoms indicating a return to the conditions of warfare in earlier ages I forbear (for a reason already given) to comment. It is more pleasant to note that some of the virtues which war evokes have never been seen to more advantage. Man has not under civilization degenerated in body or in will-power. The valour and self-sacrifice shown by the soldiers of all the nations have been as conspicuous as ever before. The line of heroes that extends from Thermopylae to Lucknow might welcome as brothers the warriors of to-day, while among those at home, in Britain, and in France who have been suffering the loss of sons and brothers dearer to them than life itself, there has been a dignity of patience and silent resignation worthy of Roman Stoics or Christian saints.

In these and other similar ways we see many a feature of human character, many a phase of political or religious life recorded by historians, verified by present experience. We can better understand what nations become at moments of extreme peril and supreme effort; and those of us who occupy ourselves with history find it profitable to note the Present for the illumination of the Past.

But the Future makes a wider appeal. Every one feels that after the war we shall see a different world, but no one can foretell what sort of a world it will be. We all have our fancies, but we know them to be no more than fancies, for the possibilities are incalculable. Nevertheless it is worth while for each of us to set down what are the questions as to the future which most occupy the public mind and his own mind.

Will the effect of this war be to inflame or to damp down the military spirit? Some there are who believe that the example of those states which had made vast preparations for war will be henceforth followed by all states, so far as their resources permit, and that everywhere armies will be larger, navies larger, artillery accumulated on a larger scale, so that whatever peace may come will be only a respite and breathing-time, to be followed by further conflicts till the predominance of one state or one race is established. Other observers of a more sanguine temper conceive that the outraged sentiment of mankind will compel the rulers of nations to find some means of averting war in the future more effective than diplomacy has proved. Each view is held by men of wide knowledge and solid judgment; and for each strong arguments can be adduced.

The effects which the war will have on the government and politics of the contending countries are equally obscure, though every one admits they are sure to be far-reaching. Those who talk of politics as a science may well pause when they reflect how little the experience of the past enables us to forecast the future of government, let us say in Germany or in Russia, on the hypothesis either of victory or of defeat for one or other of the Allied groups.

Economics approaches more nearly to the character of a science than does any other department of inquiry in the human as opposed to the physical subjects. Yet the economic problems before us are scarcely less dark than the political. How long will it take the great countries to repair the losses they are now suffering? The destruction of capital has probably been three or four times as great during these last eleven months as it ever was before in so short a period, and it goes on with increasing rapidity. It took nearly two centuries for Germany to recover from the devastations of the Thirty Years' War, and nearly forty years from the end of the Civil War had elapsed before the wealth of the Southern States of America had come back to the figures of 1860. One may expect recovery to be much swifter in our days, but the extinction of millions of productive brains and hands cannot fail to retard the process, and each of the trading countries will suffer by the impoverishment of the others.

This suggests the gravest of all the questions that confront us. How will population be affected in quantity and in quality? The birth-rate had before 1914 been falling in Germany and Britain: it had already so fallen in France as only to equal the death-rate. Will the withdrawal of those slain or disabled in war quicken it? and how long will it take to restore the productive industrial capacity of each country? Nearly all the students and younger teachers in some of our universities have gone to fight abroad, and many of these will never return. Who can estimate what is being lost to literature and learning and science from the deaths of those whose strong and cultivated intelligence might have made great discoveries or added to the store of the world's thought? Those who are now perishing belong to the most healthy and vigorous part of the population, from whom the strongest progeny might have been expected. Will the physical and mental energy of the generation that will come to manhood thirty or forty years hence show a decline? The data for a forecast are scanty, for in no previous war has the loss of life been so great over Europe as a whole, even in proportion to a population very much larger than it was a century ago. It is said, I know not with how much truth, that the stature and physical strength of the population of France took long to recover from the losses of the wars that lasted from 1793 till 1814. Niebuhr thought that the population of the Roman Empire never recovered from the great plague of the second century A. D., but war has a more distinctive potency, for where it is disease that reduces a people, it is the weaker who die, while in war it is the stronger. Our friends of the Eugenics Society are uneasy at the prospect for the belligerent nations. Some of them are trying to console themselves by dwelling on the excellent moral effects that may spring out of the stimulation which war gives to the human spirit. What the race loses in body it may — so they hope — regain in soul. This is a highly speculative anticipation, on which history casts no certain light. As to the exaltation of character which war service produces in those who fight from noble motives, inspired by faith in the justice of their cause, there can be no doubt. We see it to-day as it has often been seen before. But how far does this affect the non-combatant part of each people? and how long does the exaltation last? The instance nearest to our own time, and an instance which is in so

far typical that the bulk of the combatants on both sides
were animated by a true patriotic spirit, is the instance
of the American War of Secession. It was felt at the
time to be almost a moral rebirth of the nation. I
must not venture here and now to inquire how far the
hopes then expressed were verified by the result: for
such an inquiry would detain you too long.

These are some of the questions which it may be
interesting to set down as rising in our minds now, in
order that the next generation may the better realize
what were the thoughts and anxieties of those who
sought, *sine ira, metu, studio,* to comprehend the larger
issues of this fateful time. It is too soon to hope to
solve the problems that are crowding upon us. But
we can at least try to see clearly what the problems are,
and to distinguish between the permanent and the
temporary, the moral and the material causes that have
plunged mankind in this abyss of calamity: and we can
ask one another what are the forces that may help to
deliver it therefrom. This is a time for raising questions, not for attempting to answer them. Before some
of them can be answered, most of us who are met here
to-day will have followed across the deep River of For-
getfulness those who are now giving their lives that
Britain may live.

CHAPTER VI

A YEAR ago, in the annual Presidential Address, I mentioned and commended to your reflection a number of phenomena which the war had displayed and which deserved to be noted by historians, because they cast light on divers features of previous wars. To-day I will refer to some other such facts; and, in mentioning these, will endeavour to observe that well-settled rule which in this Academy forbids references to questions of current politics. It is a wholesome rule, for one who should depart from it might easily be betrayed, under the influence of a natural passion, into words that would afterwards be regretted.

One of these phenomena is the shock given to the rules of international law. Some of the principles that had been thought best established have been virtually destroyed. To use an Aeschylean phrase, they have been " pierced with as many wounds as a net." It has become clear that there are Governments which, when they see advantage to be gained by taking a certain course, will not be deterred from it by rules of morality or law. Nations, and especially the Powers that are neutral, are asking whether there is any use in passing such rules unless some method can be devised for enforcing them. Is it worth while, when the war has ended, to attempt a reconstruction of the fabric of international law unless it can be rebuilt upon far firmer foundations? In war time, it is only the action of neutrals that can effectively punish a belligerent transgressor. Is there any reason to look for such action? One series of breaches in that law is especially deplorable. The respect for the rights of non-combatant civilians which had been consecrated by many years of practice, and which represented the greatest mitigation of the savagery inherent in war that the progress of civilization had effected, has now disappeared. We seem to have gone back to the brutality of the earlier Middle Ages. May this be partly due to the system of what is called " The Nation in Arms "? If all the men of a country are set to fight, do they form the habit of thinking not only of all the men but also of the women and children in enemy countries as enemies to whom no mercy is to be shown? and are they disposed, when they enter an enemy country, to treat these civilians as their personal foes? With the increase of such cruelties hatred also has grown. It is fiercer between the warring peoples than ever before. In both these respects our own soldiers, and those of France and Italy, have (as we believe) been so far blameless. But one must desire that the strain should not last too long.

The power of a Government to keep its subjects in ignorance of the facts of a war, political as well as military, has never seemed so complete. This is all the more wonderful in days when the means of learning facts through the press are so much more abundant than ever before. It is a regrettable fact, because it prevents the public opinion of a people from acting as it ought upon its Government. A remarkable instance of this ignorance came lately to our knowledge. No single incident of the last two years has made so great an impression as the destruction by a torpedo of the passenger ship *Lusitania*. Now a medal was struck in Germany, and has been widely distributed there — whether or no by the German Government I have been unable to ascertain — which represents the *Lusitania* sinking in the ocean. Her fore part is piled high with cannons and aeroplanes and other war material. Here, moreover, we see a warning given to the historian who has been apt to rely upon the evidence of works of art contemporaneous with the events they depict. Suppose that five centuries hence few other records of the events of May 1915 have survived, and that this medal is then dug up from some ruin. It would be appealed to as affording the best kind of proof that the *Lusitania,* which carried no cannons and no aeroplanes, was a vessel not only laden, but conspicuously overladen with munitions of war.

There has never before been a conflict in which such efforts were made by belligerents to win the favour of neutrals. Able agents have been employed and immense sums expended in attempts to form public opinion through the Press. Such efforts have of course been primarily directed towards inducing neutrals to take some measure either positively friendly to the belligerent Power conducting the propaganda or to dissuade it from some measure helpful to that Power's enemies. In this, however, there is implied a tribute to the importance of the opinion of the world at large, and a recognition of the fact that there is such a thing as a moral standard which a nation, even if it deems itself absolved by the law of State necessity from obedience to such a standard, knows to constitute the basis whereon the judgment of neutrals, and of posterity, will be founded.

The ethical problems which this war has raised are not new, but in their essence, and sometimes even in their form, at least as old as the fifth century B.C., when we find them discussed in ancient Athens. But they have been presented on a larger scale, and in a sharper way, than perhaps ever before, and the differences between the standard recognized as applicable to the individual and that fit to be prescribed for the State have been, in one country, worked out more thoroughly as parts of a general system of doctrine. It is now asked, Have states, in their international relations, any morality at all? or are they towards one another merely like so many wild beasts, owning no obligations of honour or good faith? Is self-preservation the highest law of a State's being, entitling it to destroy its neighbour whenever it conceives this to be the easiest way to save itself? If the State has any conscience, any morality, what is that morality? How far does it differ from the moral principles which are either embodied in the law, or recognized by the opinion of each community as applicable to individual citizens within a state? If state morality is lower than the morality of the individual, ought it to be raised; and if so, how can it be raised?

If there has been a retrogression, can this be connected with the substitution of the State as an impersonal entity for the monarch as a person? In the sixteenth century the monarch, if he was not personally a base creature, had a certain sense of honour, and was amenable not only to the censures of the Church but to the dictates of chivalry, which, though chivalry never was quite what romancers have painted it, had still a certain influence. When the Emperor Charles the Fifth put himself in the power of Francis the First of France, who had been his enemy (and indeed his prisoner) before, and was to be his enemy again, he reckoned, and not in vain, upon that sense of chivalry. Francis himself was not the best kind of knight, but he had been the sovereign and the friend of Bayard, the pattern of all knightly virtue. Is any trace of that spirit of chivalry left in our time? Or do those who now administer a state feel themselves to be like the soulless directors of an incorporated company, as compared with the individual landlord or employer of former days, who recognized a sort of quasi-feudal responsibility for those who tilled his lands or worked at his bidding?

All these are serious questions, and serious not for states only, seeing that the individual may come to think that the morality (or want of it) which is good enough for the State is good enough for himself.

From noting these phenomena I pass on to a still wider question.

The awful scale of the present war, both in its local extension over the globe and in the volume of ruin and suffering which it is causing inevitably suggests the question: Is this " latest birth of Time " to be taken as the last result of civilization? Must we contemplate catastrophes such as that we now see as being likely from time to time to recur? Is a future of incessant hatred between peoples, or groups of peoples, disposing them to inflict economic injury on one another in time of peace, and breaking out from time to time in efforts to destroy one another in time of war, the future to which mankind, far more numerous than ever before, and better provided than ever before with every material comfort and luxury, must henceforth look forward?

This is a question which has been constantly present to our minds for the last two years. It includes three points fit to be considered:

1. What have been the chief causes of war in the past? Are they diminishing or increasing? Will they further diminish or increase?

2. Are there any and what forces discernible that may tend to counterwork the causes which lead to war, and, if so, are these forces that work for peace likely to grow?

3. Can any international machinery be contrived calculated to reduce the strength of the forces that make for war and to strengthen those that make for peace?

As you have all been reflecting on these questions, it is not likely that I shall be able to suggest any new facts or thoughts which may not have already crossed your minds. All I can do is to try to construct a sort of framework into which your ideas may be fitted, or, in other words, to bring up for examination certain specific points, so that definite issues may stand out and thinking be so far clarified.

In following the stream of history downwards 'from its dim and distant sources, one finds it to be a record of practically incessant fighting. Some races are fiercer than others. But War is the rule, Peace the rare exception. To the Greeks war seemed the natural relation between states. So it had been before, so it has been since. Tribes fought, cities fought, despotic monarchies fought, tiny republics fought, as vast empires are fighting to-day. This was so from the very beginning of our records. The monuments of Egypt and Assyria are devoted to war and to worship — generally to both, for the warrior king is represented as aided by the national gods who give him victory and receive their share of the spoils. So it was down through the ancient world and through the Middle Ages.

Intervals of peace have been longer within the last two centuries, especially in Europe; but the wars that preceded and followed such intervals have been on a more terrible scale than those of earlier times. The wars of the French Revolution and those of Napoleon covered twenty-three years, with two very short respites.   Since 1852 Europe has seen eight wars; and if there be added to these other wars in Asia, Africa, and America, not to speak of civil conflicts (one of which, in the United States, lasted four years), very few years can be found in which the clash of arms was not somewhere heard.   Thus there is abundant material for enumerating the causes of war.

These causes may be classed as arising either out of material interests or out of sentiment.   In most cases both causes have been operative, though often in unequal measure.

The causes of the former class include:

The desire for plunder, including the capture of women.

The desire for land or new settlements, as when the Teutonic tribes entered the Roman Empire in the fifth century and the Slavonic tribes in the sixth and seventh.

Disputed successions, in which two or more claimants to a throne have dragged their subjects or followers, and sometimes other States also, into the strife.

Interests in the sphere of commerce and industry, as when one state desires to debar another from the trade of a region (as Spain tried to debar the English from South America), or to reduce another state to commercial vassalage, as Austria did in the case of Serbia. By a curious irony, wars of commerce were often waged in a total ignorance of economic principles, and when success had been won, it proved to be worthless.

To the other class, where the motive is one of passion or sentiment, may be assigned the following causes of war:

Revenge for some injury to a people or insult to a

sovereign, or perhaps only for some defeat suffered in a previous conflict.

The desire of a monarch to win glory.

Religious animosity.

National animosity, due to previous quarrels, and perhaps increased by racial dislike.

Sympathy (usually grounded on religious or racial affinities) with a section of the subjects of another state who are believed to be oppressed by it.

National pride or vanity.

Fear of an attack by another state. This includes what are called Preventive Wars, where a Power which thinks (or professes to think) itself endangered by the designs of another Power seeks to anticipate those designs by striking first.

Few wars can be referred entirely to one cause, and the presence of any one ground for collision naturally tends to intensify the influence of such other grounds as may exist.

Of these causes there is only one which has been almost eliminated. This is religious (or ecclesiastical) hatred. The desire to propagate a faith by the sword is no longer strong even in Islam, though attempts have been recently made by the German Government as the ally of the Young Turks to utilize the preaching of a *Jihad* against the infidel. Among the so-called Christian States, religious antagonism survives only as a secondary source of enmity, disposing to civil strife or international hostility communities which have been permeated by the traditions of ancient persecution. The sentiment of ecclesiastical unity has, moreover, sometimes contributed to strengthen the sense of a national unity, leading a people to believe in what it calls its mission, and to seek to accomplish that mission by forcible means.

The old desire for territory or booty has now passed from cattle-lifting on land and Vikingry at sea into the form of a desire for more and better colonies, and for a fuller control of the means of production and of the industrial high roads of commerce. The tribal chieftain's thirst for fame appears in the desire to maintain the grandeur of a dynasty. But the ancient motives — selfishness, rapacity, and vanity — are as strong as ever. In one sense they are even more formidable, because they are often shared by the masses of a nation, and inflamed by an agency more pervasive than any that existed before the telegraph had been added to the printing-press.

Is there any one of these causes the disappearance whereof can be expected?

Religious passion has cooled, and ecclesiastical antagonisms may vanish, for the hold of dogmas and church organizations on men's minds has grown weaker. Yet the sort of fervour which expressed itself through those antagonisms, the desire in bodies of men to make other men think as they do, and so to resort to persecution if persuasion fails, may pass into new forms, and in them be again terrible. Of the other causes there is none which we have not seen active in our own time, some perhaps more active than ever before. Nearly all have, as affecting one or other of the now belligerent Powers, borne a part in bringing about the present conflict. It is the gloomiest feature in the situation that to-day the interests and passions of peoples, and not merely those of monarchs or oligarchies, are engaged, for the enmities thus created are more lasting and pernicious. In the old days when philosophers used to ridicule the whims of a king who went to war to revenge a sneer or to provide an appanage for a younger son, the king might be appeased, and the war was sometimes closed by a royal wedding, but now the bitterness which conflict engenders remains to keep jealousy and suspicion alive for many a year. As Mephistopheles says in Goethe's *Faust*, " the little god of the world bears always the same stamp." Other things change. Knowledge increases and wealth increases, but human nature has remained, in essentials, much what it was thirty centuries ago, and is never free from the risk of a relapse into the primal passions which Vanity and Ambition may so possess a whole people as to suspend the control of reason.

It may be argued that we must not lay too much stress on the circumstances attending the outbreak of the present war, for the position was unprecedented, and the conduct of some at least of the belligerents is not to be construed as indicating a bellicose spirit. This argument has force, for it is not merely the action of each nation that has to be regarded, but also the temper and motives which determined that action. But after making all allowances, the conclusion must be that the forces whence conflicts spring have never shown themselves stronger than in our own time. There is no sign of a diminution either in the spirit of rapacity or in the spirit of arrogance which moves those in whose hands lie the issues of war and peace, be they sovereigns or subjects. The sentiment of nationality, which in the days of Mazzini was deemed an almost unmixed good, has shown (and notably in South-Eastern Europe) that it can be darkened by national selfishness, jealousy, and pride.

So far, then, this brief review of the causes of war in the past gives little ground for hope.

We may now pass to the second question. Assuming, as the facts seem to indicate, that the causes which have induced war through the whole of history are still present and potent, can we discover any forces already counterworking them, and likely to strengthen in the future the motives that make for peace?

Four such forces have at various times inspired hope.

One is Religion. Of the three great World Religions, one, Islam, is essentially warlike, for it is the duty of every Musulman ruler to propagate the Faith by the sword. The other two are nominally pacific. Into the history of Buddhism I will not enter, except to remark that its practice has in all matters of State fallen so far short of its theory that theory has virtually counted for nothing. As to Christianity, it is enough to look back over the centuries since the Emperor Constantine. *Res ipsa loquitur.* What would be the thoughts of one of the Apostles, or of a martyr saint of the second century, who, revisiting this planet to-day, should be told that the gospel he preached had overspread the world, and was taken as their rule of life by nearly all of the nations on whose strife he looked down?

Are Christian principles more likely to influence the conduct of nations in the future than they have influenced it in the past? That question is as dark to-day as ever it was before. The lesson of ecclesiastical even more than of secular history is that the movements of thought and emotion and the changes they undergo are altogether unpredictable. Where there is an unlimited field of possibilities there is of course room for hope. Christianity is no doubt, at least in some countries, far more of an influence making for peace than it was four centuries ago. How little it was doing for peace even before the great religious schism of the sixteenth century had supplied a new cause for war may be seen by referring to the book (the *Complaint of Peace*) in which Erasmus comments on the unchristian spirit of his own time.

Another such force is democratic government. We are often told that so soon as the masses of the people — that is, the numerical majority of the voters — obtain in each nation the full control of its policy towards other nations, the old dynastic traditions that have so often prompted aggression will be eliminated, and the power of the military castes be destroyed. It is a gain for peace that those traditions and those castes should disappear, and no doubt that the working people have heretofore, though not indeed in this war, had more to lose by war than any other class, for they were the first to suffer in loss of employment as well as by slaughter in battle. That sense of class solidarity which has gone further among the wage-earners than in any other section of a nation — even if not nearly so far as had been expected — may dispose them to refrain from indulging in permanent hatred towards another people. Against this view it is urged — apart from the difficulty which no democracy has overcome, of finding a method by which the control of foreign relations may be exercised by the masses — that the multitude is just as liable to be swept away by passion, just as liable to be puffed up by national or racial pride, just as likely to covet the land or the commerce of other nations, as is any other class in the community. These things were seen in the popular governments of antiquity, and seen also in the (far less popular) republics of mediaeval Italy. The experience of modern democracy has been too short to warrant positive conclusions. The two countries most pacific in spirit are free democratic republics, but Switzerland has geographical as well as moral or philosophical reasons for

keeping out of war, and the United States were, between 1783 and 1914, engaged in three wars, none of
which can be called necessary, and one of which (that
with Mexico in 1845) is now admitted, by Americans
themselves, to have been scarcely justifiable. The
sources of war are to be found not in constitutional
arrangements but in human nature. They are ethical
rather than political.

A third line of argument has been used to show that
the extension of commerce, unfettered by any tariffs
giving an advantage to the domestic producer, must
give each country a larger interest in keeping the peace,
because trade is profitable both to the seller and to the
purchaser. The more trade the more profit, and
therefore the stronger is the motive for continuing the
exchange, and the wider are the opportunities for
friendly intercourse and reciprocal knowledge.

This theory also has much to recommend it. Those
who realize that they will lose by war ought to desire
peace. But the doctrine which favours a free inter-
change of products has not in fact spread or thriven of
late years. It appears to be less popular now, even in
its ancient British home, than it was fifty years ago,
which may indeed be said of the theory of *laissez-faire*
generally. Most peoples, even the formerly self-help-
ful peoples, seem disposed to look more and more to
governments to take charge of their affairs and to
make the prosperity of individuals.

Fourthly, those who see that in some countries the
increase in the functions of government and the tendency to sacrifice the individual to the State have been
accompanied by the development of a martial and aggressive spirit, conceive that the two things are naturally connected. When the State labours to increase
the wealth of individual producers by the imposition of

tariffs, and by helping its financiers to lay their grasp upon foreign countries, it is expected to go further and acquire new territories, especially if they be rich in minerals, and to open up or even create new markets outside Europe. It is only by military strength that such plans can be carried out. Hence — so the argument runs — militarism becomes popular with the great employers of labour, perhaps even with the employees. Military glory and the prosperity of the State are identified. Huge armaments are advocated for business reasons; and a people proud of its military resources is naturally tempted to use them. If, therefore, this doctrine of State omnipotence could be discredited, if the masses of a nation could be induced to revolt against the dominance of State officials and the extension of State activity, the antagonism of nations would be softened and a fertile cause of war be reduced.

This reasoning finds support in recent experience, but there are at present few signs of any general revolt against the doctrines which the argument seeks to discredit. On the contrary, the range of State action tends, in almost every country, to be increased, various classes desiring it for their own special reasons, and a well-marked current of thought running in that direction. This fact is far from proving that mankind will ultimately be the gainer. There are flood-tides of error as well as of truth, history furnishes many an instance in which such currents, strong for a while, and sweeping everything before them, have in the long run men who brought more evil than good.

Lastly, there are those who believe that we may look for the growth over the civilized world of a sentiment of friendliness and goodwill for men as men, irrespective of national distinctions, and that this sentiment will ultimately draw the peoples of the earth together and make them realize the conception of a great Common-wealth embracing all mankind, to which all will owe an allegiance higher than that which they bear to their own State and country.   To create such a sentiment was of course part of the message of Christianity: and the sentiment has always found its chief support in re-ligious belief.   But as it may exist, and has in some minds existed, apart from Christianity, it deserves to be separately mentioned.   Is the sentiment likely to grow till it becomes strong enough to influence national policy?   Has it, in fact, been growing?

To those of us who can look back for sixty years, it seems to be weaker now in most, perhaps in all, coun-tries than it was then, as it was stronger then than it had been in the days when the horrible African Slave Trade was deemed an asset in commercial prosperity. But a lifetime is far too short a period from which to draw conclusions on such a matter.   Within our own time we have seen among ourselves a great advance in the sense of responsibility felt by those to whom For-tune has been kind for those whom she has neglected. We note a more active sympathy and, despite class an-tagonisms, a stronger sense of brotherhood between the members of the same people.   May not such a feeling spread into the wider field of international relations? We perceive that in the English-speaking countries, of which alone we can judge, there exists already a warmer and more general pity than was ever seen before for suffering of every kind in every country; and wherever over the world a cry is raised for help to the victims of some disaster by earthquake, flood, or storm, the response is prompt and generous.   That the hatreds and horrors conspicuous to-day grieve us all the more because they seem to be a reversion to a dark and cruel past, is of itself a testimony to the progress which mankind had made, and raises in some minds the hope that the horrors we have been witnessing may be transient and the next change be for the better.

After thus enumerating these natural causes, if one may so call them, which have made or are making for war or for peace, it remains only to ask what prospect there is that the nations may by a conscious and united effort succeed in establishing some machinery whereby the likelihood of future wars may be at least diminished. No one can examine the wars that have sprung from the causes I have enumerated without perceiving that in the great majority of instances peace might have been kept, without dishonour to either party, and with material advantage to both, had there been more foresight of the consequences of war, and a real desire to avoid it. Many wars have been unjust, most have been unnecessary. Can any means be devised whereby the action of nations other than those two (or more) between whom the quarrel arises can be invoked to prevent the disputants from settling it by arms?

This is a very old problem. It was debated in the fourteenth century, when two great Italians, Dante Alighieri and his younger contemporary Marsilius of Padua, both saw in the authority of the Roman Emperor the guarantee, and indeed the only guarantee, for the peace of a distracted world, as others had before their time found it in the spiritual jurisdiction of the Roman Bishop. Five centuries later the problem was again discussed by Immanuel Kant, and, a generation later, a feeble attempt at a solution was made by the Holy Alliance, on principles which would have foredoomed it to failure, even had the three despotic governments of Austria, Russia, and Prussia been more altruistically minded than they were.

Both here and in the United States sanguine minds

are now busy with plans which propose some kind of federation or league or alliance of nations charged with the duty of compelling disputant Powers to refer their disputes to arbitration or conciliation, and to abstain from violent measures, at least until these peaceful methods have had their chance. Such ideas cannot be dismissed as visionary, since they have been blessed both in this country and in the United States by the highest authorities in public life. I do not propose here to discuss them, but may properly supplement what has been said regarding the causes of war by indicating what are the difficulties which all such schemes for the prevention of war have to surmount.[1]

I will mention a few of these.

That statesmen of the old school will dislike new methods which may withdraw from them some of the control they have hitherto enjoyed must be expected. But far more serious is the deep-rooted unwillingness of every nation, and especially of a strong and proud nation, to submit any part of what it calls its rights to the decision of an external tribunal. This has been happily overcome in some recent instances, but in none of those instances were the interests involved of great moment: and even in the countries where arbitration has won most favour there is a feeling, hard to overcome, that the cession of territory is a question on which the country itself must always have the last word. In every nation the fact that statesmen and journalists seek to please their public by constantly asserting the righteousness of its own cause makes it hard to arrange reasonable compromises. An American statesman, than whom there is none wiser anywhere, recently observed that one of the greatest difficulties the negotiator of a

[1] Some aspects of this topic are treated more fully in Chapter VIII., "On a League of Nations."

treaty has to encounter is the displeasure of his fellow-countrymen at any concession, even when he feels his own cause to be none too strong, and believes his country would gain by the removal of friction. Nations seem to be as sensitive on what is called the " point of honour " as were members of the *noblesse* in France and England three centuries ago. They hold out against arrangements which individual men would accept. He who suggests the dropping of a doubtful claim is accused of timidity or want of patriotism.

When a nation is invited to reduce its defensive armaments in the faith that the other states which are uniting themselves in a Peace League will join their forces with its own to repel any aggression, doubts will arise whether the parties to any alliance for the preservation of peace can be trusted to fulfil their respective obligations except when it is their obvious interest to do so. Where several allied states are alike threatened by a powerful enemy, a regard for their safety will doubtless require them to hold together. But cases may easily be imagined in which some members of the League, having at a given moment nothing direct to gain by supporting a threatened ally, may, either through unwillingness to fight or through the offer of some advantage for themselves, be induced to find a pretext for standing aside. As soon as one member thus falters, some other member is likely to follow the example, alleging that if one or more fail to stand by the obligation, the rest cannot be expected to fulfil it. The ultimate benefit to all of mutual protection and of the repression of any disturbance of the general peace may be admitted. But in politics the avoidance of a near evil is usually preferred to the attainment of a more remote good, for all can recognize the former and only those of large minds and long views can appreciate the latter.

Another difficulty has received little notice, because those who start these schemes, rejoicing in the excellence of their aim, sometimes forget to examine the means. It is the difficulty of securing persons competent to discharge the functions of Arbitration and Conciliation. Jurists versed in international law can be found fit to determine questions of a purely legal nature, such, for instance, as the interpretation of a treaty. Though there are not many such men in Europe, there may be enough for present needs. But the causes which most frequently lead to hostilities are not of a legal character. In comparatively few cases out of all those in which disputes have led to war in Europe since 1815 could the judicial methods of an arbitral court have been profitably used.[1] War usually springs from questions of wider range, questions to which no precedents are precisely applicable, questions which involve the passions of rulers or of peoples. To these questions it is Conciliation, not Arbitration, that must be applied; and the conciliators who are to deal with them must be men possessing an intimate knowledge of European politics and a long experience in international statesmanship. They must enjoy a reputation extending beyond their own country, and such as will add weight to their opinions. They must, moreover, possess sufficient independence and courage to follow their own views of what is right and wise at the risk of displeasing their countrymen. Few are the persons in whom these qualifications will be likely to meet.

It is better to state and face these obstacles than to ignore them with the complacent optimism which mis-

1 The controversy as to the succession to the duchies of Schleswig and Holstein which arose on the death of Frederick VII. of Denmark is such an instance. In that case the parties did not wish to arbitrate.

takes its own wishes for facts, or assumes that ethical
precepts will prevail against the bad habits of many
generations. But the obstacles are not insuperable.
If the free peoples of the world really desire permanent
peace, desire it earnestly enough to make it a primary
object and to forgo some of their own independence
of action to attain it, the thing may be tried with a fair
prospect of success. What is needed is the creation,
not only of a feeling of allegiance to humanity and of
an interest in the welfare of other nations as well as
one's own — what in fact may be called an International or Supra-national Mind — but also of an International Public Opinion, a common opinion of many
peoples which shall apply moral standards to the conduct of other nations with a judgment biased less than
now by the consideration of the particular national interests which each nation conceives itself to have.

Could such a moral *iudicium orbis terrarum* be established, it might do more than any arbitral tribunal, or
Council of Conciliation, or combination of Powers to
raise the level of conduct in international relations and
restrain the selfish passions even of monarchs or dema-
gogues. Though the nations are still some considerable way from the general diffusion of such a feeling
and opinion, we need not assume that the waves of passion will continue to run so high as they do now, and
we may even venture to hope that the sentiment of a
common devotion to the common welfare of all mankind will, within the next few generations, gradually
assert its strength.

This leads me to one more topic proper to be here
referred to.

In comparison with all the other sadnesses of this
time, with the sorrow and mourning that have entered
every home, with the loss of those bright young spirits

who would have been the leaders of the next generation, some among them minds that would have rendered incomparable services to learning and science and art — in comparison with these things the evil I am about to mention may seem small. Yet it is one that must be mentioned, for it directly affects the objects for which this Academy exists, and we, together with our friends and colleagues of the Royal Society, are those who best know how grave it is. I speak of the severance of friendly relations between the great peoples of Europe, the interruption of all personal intercourse, and of that co-operation in the extension of knowledge and the discovery of new truth from which every people has gained so much. The study of philosophy and history has done little for those of us who pursue it if it has not extended their vision beyond their own country and their own time, pointing out to them that human progress has been achieved by the united efforts of many races and many types of intellect and character, each profiting by the efforts of the others, and also reminding them that for further advance this co-operation is essential. To restore it is at this moment impossible. But let us at least do nothing to retard its return in happier days. Those days some of us cannot hope ever to see. For the elder men among us there has come a perpetual end of that delightful and mutually helpful companionship which united us with the learned men of two other great nations, a sense of partnership between those who pursued truth which overrode all national jealousies, and was fruitful for the progress of letters and science. This partnership is gone, and the world will for years to come suffer from its departure. Yet the severance cannot last for ever. When a storm has levelled the forest or a waterspout has scarred the slopes of a valley, the eternal forces of Nature, slow and often imperceptible in their working, but restlessly active, begin to repair the ruin the storm has wrought. Young trees spring up to renew the forest, and verdure clothes once more the devastated hillsides.

Two years ago the Spirit of Sin and Strife was let loose upon the earth like a destroying whirlwind. That spirit is personified in the *Iliad* as Até, the Spirit of Evil that takes possession of the soul. She is the power that strides swiftly over the earth, kindling hatred and prompting men to wrong. But the poet tells us that after Até came the Litae, gentle daughters of the Almighty, who, by their entreaties, soften men's hearts to pity. Halting are their steps and their visage wrinkled, and their look askance, but they bring repentance and they assuage the passions which the Spirit of Wrong has kindled. Até has been afoot in the world, and we see everywhere her deathful work. But after a time the Litae, following slowly in her track, will begin to heal the wounds she has cut deep into men's souls. Nations cannot be enemies for ever. The time must come when a knowledge of the true sources of these calamities will, even there where hatred is now strongest, enlighten men's minds and touch their hearts. May that time come soon!

Αἴλινον αἴλινον εἰπέ, τὸ δ' εὖ νικάτω.

CHAPTER VII

THE PRINCIPLE OF NATIONALITY AND ITS APPLICATIONS

SEVENTY years ago many an active and sanguine mind in Europe and America was aflame with what then began to be called the Principle of Nationality. Those were the days when Despotism seemed the great enemy to human progress and human happiness; and despotism was worst where the despot ruled over an alien people. So the sympathy, both of America and of Britain, or at least of British Liberals (among whom was then to be found a great majority of the men of light and leading), went out when, in 1848, the crash of the Orleans Monarchy in France had shaken most European thrones, to the Italian revolutionaries, to the Polish revolutionaries, to the Czechs in Bohemia, to the Magyars in Hungary, who, under the illustrious Kossuth, were fighting in 1849 for their national rights against Hapsburg tyranny, to the German patriots who were trying to liberalize Prussia and the smaller kingdoms, and bring all Germans under one free constitutional Government. Men hoped that so soon as each people, delivered from a foreign yoke, became master of its own destinies, all would go well for the world. The two sacred principles of Liberty and Nationality would, like twin guardian-angels, lead it into the paths of tranquil happiness, a Mazzinian paradise of moral dignity, a Cobdenian paradise of commercial prosperity and international peace.

These bright prospects were soon overclouded. A dreary reaction followed the revolutions that ran over Europe in 1848–49. After a while the passion for liberty regained its power. Italy was set free; Louis Napoleon's bastard imperialism disappeared in 1870. In 1867 Hungary regained her constitutional rights under the leadership of Francis Deák. But the principle of Nationality has not only proved far more difficult to apply than its apostles of those days expected, but has developed dangerous tendencies then unforeseen. In not a few countries it has led to constant disquiet and frequent strife. As the wars of the later sixteenth and earlier seventeenth century were in the main wars of religion, as the wars of the eighteenth century were in the main wars of dynastic interest, so the wars of the nineteenth century mostly arose from, or were entangled with, questions of nationality. And now, in the twentieth century, we have seen the overweening nationalism of Germany become the chief source of the present war, as it was the desire of Austria to crush the nationality of Serbia that furnished the immediate cause of its outbreak. The problems which await solution when the war ends are nearly all problems that involve the claims of peoples dissatisfied with their present rulers and seeking either independence or union with some kindred race. It is therefore of the utmost importance to have clear ideas as to what Nationality means, what part it is playing in this world-conflict, whether it has contributed to a perversion of the moral sense of Germany, and, finally, in what ways and to what extent the Allied Powers can, when victorious, apply the principle it embodies. What can be done in the coming treaty of peace to satisfy the national aspirations of the peoples and bring about a more stable international situation than Europe has yet seen?

What constitutes a Nationality? and what is the difference between a Nationality and a Nation?

The popular use of the terms is vague, and any definition that can be given is likely to be either too wide or too narrow to suit the facts. How various the facts are can be shown from a few examples. A Nationality may or may not be also a Nation. The peoples of France, of Norway, of Italy are both Nations and Nationalities. The people of Great Britain are a Nation, including three Nationalities — English, Scotch and Welsh being parts of a larger British Nationality. The races and peoples of Austria-Hungary, such as Germans, Czechs, Poles, Magyars, Slovenes, are each of them either a Nationality or a part of one, but they do not form a Nation, though they are gathered into one State. The German Empire would be nearly conterminous with a German Nationality, if we were to omit from it the Slavs of Posen and West Prussia, as well as the inhabitants of Alsace-Lorraine and those of North Slesvig, both of whom disclaim the name of Germans. The Spaniards are a Nation, and though we can speak of Catalans and Basques as elements in that nation, neither Catalans nor Basques constitute a Nationality in the same sense as do the Czechs within the Austro-Hungarian Monarchy. The former are at any rate content to remain Spaniards, while the latter desire to lead an independent political life as a Nation.

What, then, makes Nationality? Not Race alone. There may be a Nationality composed of two or more races. The Swiss people is composed of three : Franco-Burgundian, Allemano-Teutonic, and Italian. Yet the Swiss Nationality is one of the strongest and most cohesive in the world. Scottish Nationality has grown up out of four kingdoms, and it was not completed till the old hostility of Highlanders and Lowlanders ended in the eighteenth century. So the Belgians are partly Flemings, partly French-speaking Walloons, but the two elements have joined to form that genuine Belgian nationality which the Germans have been trying to break in two and destroy.

Neither does a common language make, or the want of it efface, Nationality. The Alsatians before 1870 had become virtually French by nationality, though most of them spoke German. Switzerland is all one, though three languages are spoken in it. In South America the Uruguayans are of the same stock as the Argentines, and speak the same Spanish, but they are now a distinct Nationality and proud of being a distinct Nation. It is only a series of historical accidents that have made them such.

The Albanians have never had one government of their own. They are divided into tribes, often at feud with one another. Some are Muslims, some Orthodox Greek Christians, some Roman Catholics. But they are a Nationality, and are most unwilling to be merged either in a Serb or in a Greek kingdom. So just as we cannot define the term Nationality, so neither can we lay down a general rule as to what makes the thing in the concrete. But we can recognize it when we see it, and can in each case explain by the light of history how it comes to be what it is, the product of various concurrent forces, which have given to a section or group of men a sense of their unity, as the conscious possessors of common qualities and tendencies which are in some way distinctive, marking off the group from others and creating in it the feeling of a corporate life. Race is one of these forces, language is another, religion is a third, often of the greatest importance. A common literature — perhaps in the rude form of traditions and ballads in which those traditions are preserved, as in the songs of the Serbian people — all these things count. The memories of the heroes who helped to achieve liberty for Switzerland, of the perils they faced and the victories they won, have been to its people a constant stimulus to national sentiment. Even stronger, in some countries, than recollections of glory have been the recollections of suffering, of sorrows endured, and of sacrifices nobly but vainly made. Through generations cheered by few hopes, such recollections have been nourishing that sentiment among the Irish, and the Czechs, and the Serbs, and the Armenians, and the far-scattered fragments of Israel. These are cultivated races, each with a long history and a copious literature, so the sense of Nationality has been able, through the ampler expression it found therein, to become more fully developed among them than in a comparatively backward race, such as is the Albanian or the Lithuanian. And of course where that which we call the Fibre of a race is tough, the sentiment has more tenacity and more elasticity. It is a power to be reckoned with in the modern world, far stronger now than it was a century ago.

Why has it thus been gaining strength, and that at the very time when every part of the world is being drawn into closer connection with every other part, so that each is less isolated, more dependent upon others? The passion of a nation for its independence is of course old enough. Among the Scots, for instance, it was powerful from the days of the War of Independence, when the attempts of the English King Edward the First to dominate Scotland as he had conquered Wales forced the people into a union of resistance. In Portugal it brought about the revolt which severed the country from the Spanish monarchy, of which it had formed a part for sixty years. Among the Magyars it supported Francis Rákoczy in vindicating their ancient rights against the Hapsburg sovereigns. Nearly all the European nations had a national pride which expressed itself conspicuously in times of war. In most of them, however, this pride did not, in times of peace, go deep down among the middle and lower classes. They had little more than an attachment to their own ways of life and their own religion, with a corresponding distrust of foreigners and of " heretics " or " Papists," as the case might be. The two things which distinguish Nationality, as we know it, from these old familiar feelings, are comparatively recent. One is the desire of the politically divided parts of a race (or racial group united by language and traditions) to be gathered together into a single State. The Poles, who in the successive partitions of Poland had found themselves allotted partly to Russia, partly to Austria, partly to Prussia, sought to be reunited in a Polish kingdom. Italy, still more divided and parcelled out into many principalities, longed to be delivered from their misrule, as well as from Austrian tyranny, and to become a single free State. Similarly, among the South and Middle Germans, who were ruled by a far greater number of petty potentates, there arose after the War of Liberation (1813–14) a movement for bringing together all Germans, Prussians included, under one government, which should make a German nation conterminous with German nationality, restoring the unity of the old Empire as it stood in the days of the Hohenstaufen Emperors. With this movement, as well as with the aspirations of the Poles and those of the Italians, British and American Liberals were in hearty sympathy. Italy made the strongest appeal, because the Italian Risorgimento was led by a group of men eminent by elevation of character and aims, no less than by their

brilliant gifts. Among them Cavour, Mazzini, and
Garibaldi are the best remembered, but there were
many other noble figures whose names are still cherished in Italy. To-day the same desire of a nationality
divided between several governments to coalesce in one
State shows itself among both the Northern and the
Southern Slavs, among the Italians who dwell in the
Trentino under Austrian rule, among the Rumans who
inhabit parts of Transylvania and Bukovina (to the
north and west of the kingdom of Rumania).

The other recent phenomenon is the intensification
of nationalistic pride and national vanity within many
nationalities which are already independent nations,
and especially among the greatest of these. In the
seventeenth century men's minds were occupied with religious controversies, so they knew little, thought little,
and cared comparatively little about racial distinctions.
In the eighteenth century it was the sovereigns or the
" classes " that made wars with dynastic or commercial
ends in view. But after the revolutionary convulsions
that began in 1789 the mass of the people, as in each
country it began to gain power, began also to realize
itself as a Nation. The strength of the State, the size
and the wealth of the State, became sources of pride for
it. The philanthropic quality which had marked the
apostles of freedom in the later eighteenth century, the
respect professed at least, however neglected in practice, for the Rights of Man, the desire to promote the
progress of mankind as a whole which animated the
Utilitarian school, the tenderness for backward races
which appeared in the British and American Abolition-
ists — these and similar phases of opinion fell into the
background. With a more active and pervasive national self-consciousness there came a spirit of rivalry,
a desire to compete with other States for all that was

worth having,— foreign trade, territories in parts of
the world occupied by uncivilized races. With this
came a passion for powerful fleets and armies. The
aggressive tendencies which had belonged to monarcns
passed into the blood of the peoples. A sort of
" struggle for life " set in. Theories of race were
promulgated which played up to national vanity. History was invoked to prove to each people its own superiority to its rivals. Public writers and speakers sought
popularity by disparaging other nations and flattering
their own. The spirit of Nationality was no longer a
mere assertion, wholesome and legitimate, of the right
of those who felt themselves united in language and
literature, in ideas and traditions, to be also united
politically. That spirit, the satisfaction of whose
claims had from 1840 to 1870 been expected to produce brotherhood and peace as well as freedom, now
revealed itself as a source of strife and danger. It
showed a capacity for fanaticism which almost repro-
duced the phenomena of religious animosity in the sixteenth century. It had passed into an aggressive self-
assertiveness which strove for pre-eminence and recked
little of justice.

This spirit was more or less visible in all the greater
nations, and in all of them politicians tried to turn it to
their purposes. But it reached its climax in Germany,
which came latest into the rank of the nationalities that
had consolidated themselves into States. United Germany had become the strongest of European military
powers, for Russia, vast as were her territory and
population, stood far behind in intelligence and civilization. Few things in modern history are better worth
studying than the causes which have transformed the
Germany of 1864 into the Germany of 1914.

The spirit of German Nationality which had begun

to show itself about 1770, had been immensely stimulated by the War of Liberation against Napoleon, and had blazed out again in 1848, found one of its chief supports in the memories enshrined in poetry and legend of the mediaeval Romano-Germanic Empire. These memories gave a colour of sentiment and romance to the longing for national unity. They helped to form the view which other nations, and especially Englishmen, were in those days apt to take of the Germans, that they were an idealistic, unpractical, almost dreamy people, who found their chief joy in music, art, and metaphysics.

This, however, was anything but the spirit of Prussia, or at least of the class that ruled Prussia. No romance or sentiment there. All was hard, stern, practical. The traditions typical of Prussia were traditions of war and territorial aggrandizement, which dated from the victories of the Great Elector (of Brandenburg) in the beginning of the seventeenth century and gained further strength from the career of Frederick II. (the Great). He was, and remains, the most perfect expression of the Prussian spirit. He it was who gave to Prussia's aims their definite direction and stamped upon her methods the character they have never lost. Frederick was not only a successful commander, but a diligent and capable organizer. From him date the association in the Prussian mind of civil discipline and economic progress with war and conquest, the identification of the controlling power of the State with the prosperity of the submissive subject.

Prussia's leadership in the War of Liberation gave her an ascendancy over the German peoples which was able to endure, despite the jealousies of the governments of the second-class States, such as Bavaria and Saxony, and despite also the disappointment caused to the German Liberals by the repressive policy which Prussian monarchs followed in domestic affairs. In 1848 Frederick William IV. refused the invitation of the Frankfort Parliament to become German Emperor, and William I. his successor allowed Bismarck to defy the Prussian Chamber. But whatever complaints German Liberals everywhere had against Prussia, they were compelled to look to her for leadership as against the despotic and clerically obscurantist Hapsburgs. On her they still placed their hopes for turning German nationality into a unified German State. Bismarck satisfied these hopes by his three wars, against Denmark in 1864, against Austria in 1866, against France in 1870. But the price paid for the victories which created a united Germanic Empire was the extinction of the old German Liberalism. Of the children of the Liberals of 1848–1849, some passed over into the ranks of the Conservative parties, some into those of the Social Democrats. The ideals and aims of the nation were undergoing a change.

The three wars wrought this change by reviving in greater strength than ever the traditions of Frederick II. The principle of nationality had triumphed, for unity was won, but it had been won by "blood and iron." The military spirit and traditions of the Prussian monarchy were blent with those traditions of the mediaeval Empire which the rest of Germany had cherished. Frederick's conception of a military State, resting on Power, aiming at further power, imposing strict discipline and exacting unquestioning obedience in civil as well as military affairs, began to pervade the national mind, and was accepted because the State undertook to do so much for its subjects. It gave an efficient administration by which all classes profited, and it promoted foreign trade and every kind of material devel-

opment by every possible means.   The rapidly growing
industrial and commercial prosperity obtained by this
policy, and by the energy of the people, intensified the
sense of national pride and self-confidence.

The transports of joy which accompanied the victories of 1870–71 and the attainment of full national
unity in an Empire which seemed to re-embody the me-
ridian glory of the Middle Ages, stimulated — one
might almost say deified — the sentiment of Nationality, spurring the new realm to achieve fresh conquests
beyond the seas.   In the competition for unoccupied
tropical territories which began not long afterwards,
large claims were made for Germany.   The " Colonial
policy " became popular, and with it presently came the
desire for a great navy.   Bismarck, who had been content to make Germany One State, and the strongest in
Europe, was swept along by the current, and almost
compelled to acquire colonies which he did not care for.
He cared even less to turn eastward, and emphatically
disclaimed any interest in Constantinople.   But when
he was gone the young Emperor William II., professing himself the friend of Islam and of Abdul Hamid,
formed plans for dominating the Near East, and obtained first commercial and railway concessions, and
ultimately a practically controlling influence over the
rulers of Turkey.   A powerful navy was created.   The
scope of ambition enlarged itself, in many German
minds, to the domination of the world.

Nationalism, as it affected the educated class generally, made the greatness of the country seem the supreme aim for State and individual, justifying not only
aggression, but even breaches of faith, such as was the
invasion of Belgium in 1914.   *Salus Germaniae su-
prema lex.*   As the Nation had become an Army rather
than a People, Nationalism gave to the military caste a

prestige and authority never seen in Europe before. The Caste dominated politics. Bismarck had resisted it and disapproved its methods. Unscrupulous as he could be, he recognized the power of world opinion, and showed a certain respect for it by his efforts to put his antagonists, technically at least, in the wrong.[1] But he had no civilian successors of equal strength. The military and naval chiefs to whom his controlling influence passed, thinking and dreaming incessantly of war, and making Power and Victory their only aim, became so obsessed with the ideas of successful war, that morality ceased for them to exist. All methods became lawful. It was to them a duty — as it had been to the Spanish Inquisitors — to be cruel and faithless if cruelty and faithlessness promised success in their aims.

Nowhere else in the modern world have national pride and self-confidence risen to so high a pitch. Not even the Romans in the days of Augustus surveyed the world, of which they were masters, from such a pinnacle of conscious superiority, for the Romans did at least acknowledge the Greeks as their teachers, and recognized the greater brilliance of Hellenic science and literature and art.[2] But in the case of Germany several streams of feeling combined to swell the flood of pride. There was the marvellous growth of industry and commerce. There was the progress of chemistry and physics, assiduously pursued in many Universities, turned to practical ends in technical institutions, and so made to yield an ample harvest of profits to the commercial class. There was a literature not indeed equal in richness and variety to that of Britain or that of

---

1 Thus in 1864 he did not act till Denmark had broken the treaty of 1852; in 1866 he contrived that the breach of the treaty of 1865 should come from Austria. See Professor Munroe Smith's interesting book, *Militarism and Statecraft*, for an instructive comparison between Bismarck's diplomacy and that of his latest successors.

2 Cf. *Aeneid*, bk. vi; Horace, Epp. "vos exemplaria Graeca."

France, but illustrated by many great names, especially
in the domains of abstract thought.   And, above all,
there were the triumphs of the Prussian rifle and can-
non.   Much has been attributed to the histories, like
those of Giesebrecht and von Raumer, which celebrated
the achievements and virtues of mediaeval heroes, much
to the philosophical theories which have claimed omnipotence for the State and placed it above all moral obligations.   But it is Facts that have remoulded the German mind during the last fifty years.   Hegel and
Treitschke would have counted for little without the
three successful wars which have Prussianized Germany
and made War seem to so many to be the foundation
of her greatness.

While the spirit of Nationalism was running to this
excess in Germany, the small nationalities of South-
Eastern Europe and Western Asia were awakening to a
more active life.   The war of 1877–78 had delivered
Bulgaria from the Turk, the rising of the Eastern
Rumelians in 1885 enlarged its territory, and led Serbia
to attack it.   Greece and Montenegro gained exten-
sions in 1880 by the help of England.   Each of the
four Balkan nationalities [1] had its traditions and its
aspirations, and as the latter were incompatible with
those of its neighbours, a bitter rivalry followed where
there ought to have been a mutual good-will, and where
there was really a common interest, which might have
taken useful shape in a federal union against the hostility of Turkey and the dangerous patronage of Russia
and Austria.   Meanwhile, in Asia the rulers of Turkey were seeking to preserve their own national and
religious predominance by exterminating their Christian subjects.   It was the Armenians, as lying most out

---

[1] Greece, Serbia, Rumania, and Bulgaria. Montenegro, though an independent State, belongs to the " Jugo-Slav " Nationality.

of the sight and knowledge of Europe, and because
most feared in respect of their industry and intelligence,
who were the chief victims of massacre, but Greeks
and Syrians too have had to suffer.   Turkish misgov-
ernment went so far as to awaken in Syria also the
long-dormant sense of Arab nationality.

As the present war has sprung from the strife of
races and religions in the Balkan countries and from
that violence done to the sentiment of nationality in
Alsace-Lorraine which made France the ally of Russia,
so also has it raised a multitude of other questions of
nationality in various parts of Europe and Western
Asia which call for settlement at the end of the war.
Settled they must be, if the desired peace is to endure
and if the proposed League of Free Nations to Enforce
Peace is to have a fair chance of success.   These questions fall into five groups:

I. Those of Western Europe.
II. Those of East Central Europe (Bohemia, Po-
land, and the western parts of Russia).
III. Those of South-Eastern Europe (the so-called
" Balkan Countries ").
IV. Those of Western Asia (Syria, Armenia, the
Caucasus, and the Twelve Islands of the
Aegean Sea).
V. Those of West Central Asia (Persia with,
possibly, Turkestan and Siberia).

Of these Groups, Nos. III. and IV. are really one,
for both involve the fate of the Turkish Empire.   The
step preliminary to their settlement is to abolish for
ever the rule over subjects of a different faith of the
unspeakable, irreclaimable, intolerant Turk,[1] who has

---

1 By " the Turk " I mean the Osmanli as a ruler, not the Turkish peasant,

been a curse to Asia, as well as to Europe, for six centuries. But it is convenient to take the Balkan countries separately, because their fate is inwoven with that of another Empire, whose dynastic interests have caused infinite mischief since the days of the Emperor Ferdinand the Second.[1]

I. Western Europe

The West European issues of Nationality are those of Alsace-Lorraine and of the Danish-speaking population of North Slesvig, who have been kept under German rule ever since the wars of 1864–66, though it had been stipulated that they were to be restored to Denmark. These cases are too familiar to need description. The German Government has tried to create another racial question by its attempt to make the Flemings of Belgium into a Germanic nationality as opposed to the Walloon or French-speaking part of the population. But this ingenious plan, interesting as proceeding from those who have laboured to extinguish Polish nationality in Posen, did not suggest itself till after an unfortunate beginning had been made by shooting in cold blood, during the invasion of Belgium, batch after batch of innocent non-combatant Flemish burghers at Louvain, Aerschot, and other Belgian towns. Nor has it been promoted by the more recent carrying off into virtual slavery of crowds of Flemish workmen and peasants to toil in German factories or help to construct German entrenchments on the Western front.

who is usually an honest and kindly being, though capable of ferocity on occasions.

1 In briefly describing these questions I shall seldom express my own opinions, for though whoever has travelled through the countries concerned (as I have through many of them) cannot but have his opinions, views are little worth without arguments to support them, and for arguments there is no room in such a sketch as this.

II. CENTRAL EUROPE

The break-up of the Russian Empire which followed the revolution of March 1917 has created some very intricate new problems in the regions which lie between the Baltic and the Euxine, in addition to the old problems of Bohemia and Poland. Bohemia was an independent Slavonic kingdom ten centuries ago, and is a separate kingdom now, though since 1526 its crown has been worn by the Hapsburg archdukes of Austria, who have (since 1805) called themselves Emperors of Austria. Its original Slavonic quality has been affected by the influx of Germans from the North and West. These now form about one-third of the population, but the spirit of Czech nationality, which had never died out, has been powerfully reinvigorated since 1848, and most markedly so in recent years. This spirit has spread not only among the Czechs of Moravia, but also among the Slovaks of Northern Hungary, whose language is almost the same as Czech, though they have been for many centuries subjects of the Hungarian Crown. Far behind the Czechs as these Slovaks are in intellectual culture, their sense of their kinship with that race and their resentment at the attitude towards them of the Hungarian Government have produced among them a sympathy with the Czech movement, which now seeks to create a Czecho-Slovak State covering the regions aforesaid. Both Czechs and Slovaks have during this war given proof of courage and of devotion to their nationalist aims by going over in large numbers from the Austrian armies to the Russian, and by the valour with which they have fought along the Volga and in Siberia on behalf of the Entente Allies. They constitute a population which may be roughly estimated at 12 millions, and their aspirations are likely to receive general sympathy in Britain, France, and Italy, probably in the United States also.

Polish politics are too intricate and their aspects too changeful to be described here. It must suffice to say that the bulk of the Polish nation, including nearly all of those who are subjects of Prussia in Posen and West Prussia, and a large (though probably smaller) proportion of those who are subjects of Austria in Galicia and Austrian Silesia, desire to see Poland become once more an independent kingdom, if possible with the limits which it had before the lamentable partition of 1776, and at any rate with some guaranteed access to the Baltic. Whether the Ruthenian population of Eastern Galicia and parts of Russian Poland should be included in this kingdom or be assigned to the Ukraine is a moot question. The population of this reconstituted Poland would be large, perhaps from twenty-two to twenty-eight millions, that of the proposed Czecho-Slovak State something over eight millions.

When we pass from these two ancient kingdoms to the races which have been gathered into an independent State, and most of which cannot even be called Nations, Lithuanians and Letts in East Prussia and the north-western parts of Russia, Slavonic Ruthenians or Little Russians in the Ukraine, Finns in Esthonia and Finland, the difficulties to be settled at the conclusion of a General Peace become even greater. Here there are no natural boundaries either of mountains (for these regions are parts of the great East European Plain) or of rivers. Neither are there potent historic traditions moulding the wishes of the peoples. Language and religion are practically our only guides to the discovery of any nationalistic distinctions on which the building of political fabrics can be based.

The Finns, a vigorous race, have a language entirely
different from that of their Slavonic neighbours, and
they are Protestants. The Lithuanians have their
own very ancient tongue, and they are mostly Roman
Catholics. The Letts, also with a language closely
resembling Lithuanian, are mostly Protestants. A
few belong to the Orthodox Church. Neither of these
are Slavs. The Ruthenians or Little Russians, like
the less well-marked groups—hardly to be styled nationalities—called Red Russians and White Russians,
speak Slavonic dialects differing but slightly from the
much larger mass of the Great Russians, and they, as
well as the latter, belong to the Orthodox Eastern
Church. If the German Government were left to deal
with the problem which this part of Europe presents,
it would doubtless set up a number of small principalities, which it would control partly through rulers of its
own choice, partly by military menace, partly by the
use of money. The weakness of such rulers, and their
mutual jealousies, would make them helpless vassals
of the German Empire. The Western Allies, whose
aim must be not only to create a stable order, but also
to foster liberty and to respect the spirit of nationality,
promoting in an unselfish spirit the welfare of populations hitherto neglected by their despotic sovereigns,
will have a harder task, for most of these populations
can hardly be deemed fit to work democratic institutions. Politically, the Finns are most advanced, for
they have had in the Grand-duchy of Finland an autonomous government under the Czars. In some cases,
as, for instance, that of the Ukraine (Ruthenes or
" Little Russians "), we do not yet know how far what
can be called a true Nationality, *i.e.* a sense of constituting a distinct intellectual and moral entity, so far
pervades the bulk of the people as to make them desire

a distinct governmental organization. Such a sense seems to exist in a part at least of the educated class, and the Austrian and German Governments have tried to develop it in order to sever the Ukrainians from the other Russians. But is it general? The Finns of Finland, an educated and highly intelligent race, are of course in a different position. They might well be left, when the German intruder has been expelled, to form an independent Government, probably republican, perhaps a member of a Federation, which should include Esthonians, Letts, and Lithuanians. A reconstituted Poland might also be a member, but the smaller peoples may, it is believed, prefer to be left to themselves.

III. South-Eastern Europe

Here we find five distinct Nationalities — Ruman, Bulgarian, Serb, Greek, and (if the Turks can be called a Nationality) Turkish, or at any rate Muslim. Montenegro, though an independent State, is hardly a nationality, for its people are racially identical with those of Serbia, Bosnia, and Dalmatia. Each of these nationalities has claims beyond its present political boundaries.

The Rumans seek to acquire a large part of Bessarabia (included in Russia till 1917), which is inhabited by Rumans, and also most of Transylvania, with a slice of Eastern Hungary and a little bit of Bukovina. In Transylvania, however, there is a certain population of German-speaking Saxons, chiefly in a few towns such as Hermanstadt and Kronstadt, and a greater population of Magyars, the largest part of which consists of a remarkable mountain people called Szeklers, slightly differing in aspect and dialect from the Magyars of the plain, but equally unwilling to be merged in the Rumans.   How are the respective rights of these elements to be adjusted?   The Rumans also dispute with Bulgaria the possession of the territory called the Dobrudja, which lies along the Black Sea south of the lowest part of the Danube's course, and which they forced it to cede in 1913, though the bulk of its population speaks Bulgarian.   Some politicians would like to go farther south and get hold of Varna, but there is no Ruman population there to justify such a demand.

The Bulgarians, besides contesting Rumanian claims to the Dobrudja, seek to recover Adrianople and the country to the south of it as far as Constantinople, much of which is certainly Bulgar-speaking and was yielded to them by the treaty of 1912, though the Turks took it back from them during the calamitous war of 1913.   Moreover,— and this is one of the most troublesome of all the Balkan questions,— Bulgaria disputes with Serbia the possession of Southern Macedonia, *i.e.* the country west of the river Struma as far west as Monastir and Ochrida, and also disputes with Greece a strip of territory along the north coast of the Aegean.   Both of these were assigned to Bulgaria by the treaty of 1912 but lost in the war of 1913, and then ceded, the former to Serbia, the latter to Greece. Both have been reoccupied by the troops of Bulgaria in the present war, and are claimed by her on the ground that their inhabitants are predominantly of Bulgarian stock.   It was the popular desire to recover these districts which enabled King Ferdinand to lure or cajole his subjects into the war.

Not less perplexing than this set of questions are those which relate to Albania, a country which has never formed an independent State, and was till recently part of the Turkish Empire, nominally at least, for the Turks had so little effective control that I found, when travelling there in 1885, that a Turkish general, desiring to send troops across the country, found it prudent to take off the soldiers' uniforms, that they might pass through in small bodies, and so escape the unfriendly attentions of the warlike tribes. Some of these tribes indeed have maintained their practical independence ever since Illyricum was lost to the Roman Empire in the sixth and seventh centuries. The boundaries of the country which they occupy are undetermined. On the south in particular the Skipetar (as the Albanians call themselves) are mingled with a Greek-speaking population, so that it is hard to say where Greece begins and Albania ends. On the north and east there is a similar contact, though rather less intermixture, with the Serbs. Thus both Serbia and Greece advance to certain districts claims which the Skipetar would not admit. So does Montenegro also. Italy, too, has now stepped in, and is understood to desire a protectorate over parts at least of Southern Albania. An unprejudiced observer is disposed to think that the best way out of this imbroglio would be to leave the mountain tribes severely alone. They are a bold and spirited race, and would fight fiercely for the independence which they love. To subdue such a people who, like the Afghans, love fighting for its own sake and are defended by rocky fastnesses, would give far more trouble than any results to be expected could justify. There has never been among them any effective government, that is, any regular civil administration, and they get on without it. All that seems needed is to fix their boundaries — no easy task — give them access to the Adriatic, and prevent them, by a sort of police cordon, from raiding their neighbours.

Next we come to the largest problem of all, that of the Slavonic population which occupies the south-western parts of the Austro-Hungarian monarchy, viz. Bosnia and Herzegovina, Dalmatia, Istria, Croatia-Slavonia (the district south of the middle and lower course of the Drave), Carniola, Eastern Carinthia, and a district of Southern Styria. The inhabitants of the westerly parts of these regions are called Slovenes, and speak a language cognate to, but slightly different from, that of the Dalmatians and Croatians, who are all Serbs, practically identical in race with the Serbians, though differing in religion, for the latter are "Orthodox" Greek, the former, as also the Slovenes, Roman Catholics. It would appear, though no trustworthy statistics exist, that in Croatia-Slavonia the proportions of the races are: Croats, 62 (Catholics using the Latin alphabet); Serbs, 26; Germans, 5; and Magyars 4 per cent respectively. [There are said to be 40,000 Slovenes in the Italian district of Friuli.] The Bosnians are also Serbs, mostly Orthodox, though there are some Catholics, and a few Muslims remain. Taken altogether, these populations are now described as Jugo-Slavs (*i.e.* South Slavs) to distinguish them from the Northern Slavs (Czechs, Slovaks, Poles, and Ruthenes, and Russians generally).

The ambition of Serbia is to be the nucleus of a great Jugo-Slav State, embracing all these branches of the South Slavonic stock, which count some eight millions of souls, and delivering them all out of the hand of the Hapsburgs. Assuming that the power of Austria can be so completely broken as to make this aim attainable, we have to ask whether all the above-named sections of her present subjects desire their deliverance. They have had no opportunity during the war of expressing their wishes, by political methods, and they have not in war broken away from the Austrian armies as the Czechs have done. The only means hitherto

suggested for enabling them to exercise the right of
self-determination after the war is by some sort of
popular vote or so-called "plebiscite." Will their
assent be forthcoming? It used to be thought that the
ecclesiastical differences between the Roman Catholic
and the Orthodox Slavs would prevent union, but those
have come to seem smaller as the sentiment of racial
unity has grown. Though that sentiment is less developed among the Slovenes than it is in Bosnia or
Dalmatia, or perhaps in Croatia, the Jugo-Slav leaders
seem confident that it will overcome any lingering loyalty to the Hapsburgs. It must, however, be remembered that leaders, especially when they are also exiles,
naturally tend to attribute their own ardent convictions
to their fellow-countrymen at home, many of whom
may be but faintly interested in nationalistic aspirations. More cannot be said at present. If the dynasty
of Rudolf comes to a perpetual end, it may well die
unwept, for no long-descended line has, with the exception of Maria Theresa, ever shown less nobility
of soul or pursued its own interests in a more selfish
spirit than this House has done since the well-inten-
tioned Maximilian II. passed away in 1576.

An Austrian monarchy need not, however, cease to
exist when the South Slav regions have broken away
from her, and when Italy has received the Trentino
and any other districts to which she may show herself
entitled. The Hapsburgs may still keep what they
had, and rather more than what they had, in the fifteenth century, that is to say, their purely German territories, the archduchies of Upper and Lower Austria,
most of Tirol, Vorarlberg, Salzkammergut, most of
Styria, and Western Carinthia. Whether these territories will be attracted to Germany may depend on
what befalls that country after the war. Whether the

Magyars, now that they have no longer to fear that Russian autocracy whose invading hosts cut short their struggle for liberty in 1849, will care to prolong their political connection with the Hapsburgs and Germanic Austria will be their own affair. They are a high-spirited and forceful race, who could stand alone.

IV. Western Asia

Passing from Europe to Asia, we find ourselves among the Twelve Islands in the eastern part of the Aegean Sea (the so-called Dodekanese), most of which belong rather to the latter than to the former continent. They were taken from the Turks by the Italian fleet in 1912, and Italy still continues to hold them, though they were not ceded to her by the treaty of 1913. Their population is, with the exception of a few Muslims, wholly Hellenic. One of them, Astypalaea, is specially valuable in respect of its excellent harbour. What is to be done with Constantinople, unique in its position as it is in its history? There is a general feeling that a position of such incomparable military and commercial importance, guarding the passage from one continent to another, commanding the gateway to a great inland sea, ought not to be left in the hands of any Great Power. Is it then to be assigned to a weak Power, and if so, to which? Or is an attempt to be made to place it under the joint control of some combination of Powers, a hazardous experiment, which may, however, have to be tried, *faute de mieux?*

The questions that arise in connection with these two groups of nationalities (II. and III.) are so intricate that it may be well to state concisely the schemes for settling them which have, so far, received the most general support from the European Allies and from America.

As respects Central Europe, the claims of the Czechs are felt to be strong. Their fervid national sentiment, their literature and traditions, their ancient historic rights entitle Bohemia to disvalue her connection with the Hapsburgs and live once more as a separate and independent State. Difficulties will, however, arise in dealing with the German minority and in the delimitation of those districts in North-West Hungary which are purely Slovak. Not less warm is the sympathy which the free peoples of Europe and America have given to the Poles in their long struggle to recover national independence. We all desire a reconstituted Poland, strong enough to hold its own. But here, too, there are obstacles to be overcome. Where are the frontiers to be drawn on the north and east? How is access to the sea to be secured? Are the Ruthenians of Eastern Galicia to be a part of Poland, or united with their brethren in the Ukraine? Can Prussia be forced to let go Posen which she has laboured for two generations to Germanize?

The problem of European Russia is one on which few people in Western Europe or America are qualified to speak confidently, but the balance of opinion inclines to leave the Ruthenians (or Little Russians) to settle for themselves whether they wish to go with the Great Russians or to stand alone. It is clear that the Finns in Esthonia and Finland wish to be quit of Russia altogether, and this is probably the desire of the Letts and Lithuanians also. The question for these four small peoples therefore comes to be, Shall they form a group of petty unconnected States or shall they be united in a Baltic Federation?

When we turn to South-Eastern Europe the questions in debate are so many and opinion is so divided upon them that it is impossible here to do more than summarize the main points in controversy. Briefly stated, they are these:

1. Shall a Jugo-Slav State be created embracing Croats, Slovenes, and Serbs, who are now subjects of Austria, and also the Serbs of Serbia and Montenegro?

2. What possessions shall Italy have on the Adriatic coast, and

3. Shall the Albanians be independent? What ports on the Adriatic shall they receive?

4. Where shall the boundaries be drawn?

    (*a*) Between Greece and Albania?

    (*b*) Between Greece and Bulgaria?

    (*c*) Between Serbia and Bulgaria?

    (*d*) Between Serbia and Albania?

    (*e*) Between Bulgaria and Rumania?

5. How much of Transylvania, of Bukovina, and of Bessarabia shall be allotted to Rumania?

6. What shall become of Constantinople and the bit of territory behind it still left to the Turks in Europe?

Those who know even a little of these countries know that the races live so intermixed that it is impossible to draw any lines without placing many villages or even large districts of one nationality within the territory of a State of a different nationality. There must be a certain amount of give and take, but unfortunately the temper which arranges a give and take is wanting to the Balkan peoples.

In Asia Minor we find a Greek-speaking population along the west coast, mixed with Muslims in the country districts and with Armenians in the cities. On the north coast, and in the great inland plateau, the inhabitants are nearly all Muslims, calling themselves

Osmanlis, besides some Circassians and Muslim sects like the Kizil Bashes, with Greek and Armenian Christians scattered here and there, the latter chiefly in the cities and in the Cilician mountains. The principle of nationality would allot the western seaboard, with its adjacent islands, to Greece, and leave the plateau to the Muslims. If it is desired to maintain an Ottoman Sultanate, these inland and northern regions might be assigned to it. Bad as Turkish rule is everywhere, such a Sultanate would be too weak to venture to oppress or massacre the Christian inhabitants of the few cities in the regions aforesaid. For a capital it might have Afium Kara Hissar, or Konia, which was the seat of the Seljukian Sultans in the eleventh and twelfth centuries. It need hardly be said that the Western Allies will feel bound to exclude from German influence both the Caucasian countries and Mesopotamia, since the Germans have not concealed their wish to use these regions as a stepping-stone to the domination of Central Asia and the creation of a menace to the position of Britain in India.

No one will now venture to propose that the Turk should be allowed to retain any power in the countries east and south of the Taurus range, in which he has committed such unheard-of cruelties as those which Armenians and Syrians have had to suffer in 1915 and 1916. His work of massacre was unfortunately so thoroughly done in these two years that the larger part of those elements of the population on which its prosperity depended, and to which some kind of self-government might have been given, has been destroyed in Armenia and greatly reduced in Syria. The Armenian race is, however, singularly industrious and singularly tenacious of life. It quickly repairs its losses. Its sense of nationality is so strong that many who emigrated to escape the miseries from which they were suffering may return, even from the United States, where they are counted by hundreds of thousands. But these native races, progressive as they are by their intelligence and their industry, will for some time to come need a guiding and protecting hand. They live intermingled with so-called "Turkish" Muslims and with Kurds. The latter have been wont to rob and murder and carry off the women of their Christian neighbours, whom the Turkish Government tried to keep unarmed. But the Kurds were constantly stirred up and hounded on by the Government. Left to themselves, they might be kept in order by a comparatively small police force. There is little racial and no great religious hatred between them and the Armenian or Nestorian Christians. Much the same may be said of northern Syria, mainly Arabic-speaking and Christian, except in and about Aleppo and in Damascus. Armenia and Syria have great natural resources, and want nothing but a Government which will secure public order and improve communications to recover the prosperity of which a blighting rule has deprived them. The question is: What Power or Powers will undertake, in an unselfish and benevolent spirit, the task of securing order? A small gendarmerie, organized and officered by a civilized Power, would suffice, and the expenditure on roads and railways might before long prove remunerative.

What has been said of Syria applies to that region lying farther south which arouses our keenest interest. In Palestine the Muslims, speaking Arabic, have long disliked the Turks, and would welcome a European Protectorate. So, of course, would the small Christian element. The Jews, who have already established flourishing agricultural colonies, are prepared to return in numbers so large that there may be a difficulty in finding land for all who wish to come. Irrigation works would, however, vastly increase the productive areas. In the Jordan valley alone hundreds of thousands of acres could be reclaimed from aridity at no great cost, and along the coast between Carmel and Gaza large tracts could be made productive by the construction of reservoirs in the valleys which descend westward from the Judaean highlands.

Mesopotamia, which thirty centuries ago was one of the richest and most populous parts of the world, is now mostly a wilderness, over which nomad Arabs and Kurds wander at their will across broken canals and among the huge mounds which mark the sites of famous cities ruined long ago. It might again become one of the chief corn-supplying countries, not to speak of cotton and other staples. Labour is of course wanted, but under some sort of civilized Protectorate labour might soon flow in. There is here no question of nationality to deal with, the country being almost empty. Titular sovereignty might be given to the King of the Hedjaz or some other Musulman potentate. But in whom are the duties of a Protecting Power to be vested?

Turning to the north, we come again in contact with old nationalities. The middle and western parts of Transcaucasia are inhabited by the Georgian race (the ancient Iberians), to which the Mingrelians, Imeretians, and Lazes belong, the former Christian, the mountain Laz tribes (dwelling south of Batum), who are much less advanced, Mohammedan. Out of them a new State, renewing the traditions of the old Georgian monarchy, which did not finally disappear till 1800, might be created. Eastern Transcaucasia (the lower valley of the Kura River and the coasts of the Caspian) is chiefly occupied by Mohammedan Tartars, who had no sense of nationality, and indeed had not heard of the thing, till the recent Pan-Turanian propaganda of the German Government began to be applied to them. Can any State be built up out of what is not even a nation? Southern Transcaucasia, round Erivan, Kars, and Ani (the ancient capital), is part of the Armenian lands, and would naturally come within any governmental organization that may be given to them.

V

Easternmost of all among the countries which the war has shaken are Persia and its northern neighbour Turkestan, the Iran and Turan of the ancient Oriental world. It is so hard to know what to do with them that the Congress which will have to settle Europe and the fragments of Asiatic Turkey on solid foundations may well seek to avoid the task. The Khanates of Khiva and Bokhara, where Russian Bolsheviks have been fighting fiercely with Muslim Turkmans, might perhaps be left alone, though one would be sorry to see them relapse into the barbarism of ninety years ago. With Persia it is otherwise. Europeans have acquired large interests there and enterprises set on foot whose continuance would have benefited the country. It is now threatened with anarchy. The monarchy has broken down; the attempts to set up a Constitution and a Parliament seem to have failed, though the Persian people has retained its high intelligence and still from time to time produces remarkable men. Can any plan be devised by which the Allied nations could give the country a prospect of order and peace? Here, however, the questions involved are not primarily those of Nationality — and the same may be said of Siberia

— so here our survey of that particular aspect of the Resettlement of the Near Eastern World may close.

This list of questions that await decision is a long one, yet it gives no sufficient impression of their complexity and of the multitude of details a knowledge of which will be needed by those who will represent the belligerent Powers at a Peace Congress. Many points are highly controversial, and few are the well-informed persons to be consulted who add impartiality to their knowledge. The members of the Congress will need to be on their guard against journals, magazines, pamphlets, and books written to advocate the claims of particular nationalities, or particular factions within nationalities. Some of these nationalities have secured what is called " a good press." Their particular case is constantly and forcibly pushed, while the case on the other side is misrepresented or ignored, and may find hardly any organ to defend it. Thus opinion is manufactured for a public which is never given the chance of hearing all the facts fully and fairly set forth.

Another danger of which a Peace Congress will, we may hope, beware, is that of assuming responsibility for framing constitutions and erecting governments in States which the treaty of peace will call into existence. Should an Ukrainian republic, for instance, be set up or a new Jugo-Slav State be formed by the union of Bosnia and Herzegovina, perhaps of Croatian and Dalmatian districts also, with Serbia or Montenegro, it would be better to let the peoples of these regions settle for themselves their relations with one another and their form of government rather than for the treaty-making Powers to undertake the task. If the latter were to attempt it, they could hardly escape liability for maintaining and guiding the course of whatever government they had set up, a thing always full of risks for all parties concerned, and specially difficult when undertaken by a Concert of Powers. Remember the failures of the European Concert after the Treaty of Berlin in 1878. The new States so constituted or enlarged will doubtless have plenty of troubles to face, but each had better face those troubles for itself and learn by its own experience.

Many cases will arise where no arrangements can be made satisfactory to all the nationalities concerned. In Bohemia, for instance, how are the wishes of the Czech majority to be reconciled with the rights of the considerable German-speaking minority who live intermingled with the Czechs, and form in some few districts the larger part of the inhabitants? How is it to be determined whether a territory which is by race and language half Greek and half Albanian shall be dealt with? We remember the case of Ulster, in which it was found impossible to induce the contending parties to agree as to whether the counties of Tyrone and Fermanagh were or were not to be included in the area for which special treatment was proposed. Compromises are apt to be resisted on both sides. The difficulty may in some countries be lessened by the creation of local self-government for small areas. Villages belonging to the race and language which is in a minority in the country as a whole might be permitted to administer their local affairs, including churches and schools, a fertile source of quarrels. Such an expedient would reduce friction and provide some sort of safeguard against oppression by the Central Government. In South-Eastern Europe much bitterness has arisen from the attempts of the majority in the country to enforce uniformity in the use of its own language in schools, as well as in official proceedings.

Some may fear that the difficulties which the Peace Congress will find in the tremendous task of redrawing the map of Europe in accordance with the principles of Nationality and " self-determination of the peoples " will prove so great that the Congress will abandon it in despair, and cut short an interminable labour by rough-and-ready methods, leaving many aspirations unsatisfied, many injustices unredressed.   This is no idle fear. Yet every such injustice may be the parent of future unrest, perhaps of future war.   Considering how strong the sentiment of nationality has grown to be, and how earnestly the Allied peoples desire that it should cease to be a source either of domestic troubles or of international strife which would blast the prospects of a Peace League, ought not the Congress to do all that it can to respect and give effect to that principle, even though many months be required for the task?   Much, I venture to think, may be expected from the influence of the United States in the Congress, because the great republic of the West will stand impartial between the jarring interests which have hitherto affected the Governments of the European Powers in their dealing with the Near East, and because she has no selfish interests of her own to serve.   Poles, Czechs, Germans, Russians, Magyars, Serbs, Bulgars, Greeks, Rumans, Albanians, Armenians, Arabs, and Syrians will recognize in her representatives arbiters more detached and unbiassed than those of any European nation would be assumed to be.   This is an advantage which the Congress will possess over those that have preceded it, for in them, from the days of Osnabrück and Münster in 1648 down to those of Berlin in 1878, the diplomatic envoys of the Powers were sent to press the interests each of his own country, and could not help regarding at every turn those interests, unchecked by the presence of any who came to speak only for justice and liberty.

The respect to which the principle of Nationality is entitled ought to be extended to the German people also. For the German Government, indeed, no punishment could be too severe. We cannot forget its shameless perfidy and the detestable cruelty with which it has carried on war, even against non-combatants, by land and sea. It must be disgraced and discredited, fatally discredited, in the eyes of its own people by the only things that will discredit it and deliver them — failure and defeat. The military caste which rules Germany, its pernicious theories and its inhuman methods, have been a menace to the rest of mankind. That menace must be removed. But to go beyond this and try to dismember Germany, or inflict upon her any wanton humiliation, would be a capital error. The insolent arrogance which Napoleon showed when Prussia lay prostrate before him after the battle of Jena provoked the harsh retaliations of the Prussian army when it entered France in 1814, creating for the first time a deep-rooted animosity between the two peoples. The Allies had better sow no dragon's teeth out of which armies shall hereafter spring up. They may content themselves with a victory which shall vindicate the principles of Right, and deliver the world from the dangers with which German ambition has threatened it.

Nationalism, carried to an extravagant excess in Germany, became dangerous to the world when united to the doctrine of an omnipotent and non-moral State, just as two chemical substances which may be comparatively harmless apart make up a dangerous explosive when combined. But though exaggerated and perverted by the Germans in a way which no one expected sixty years ago, its spirit is innocent and useful in moderation. The same electricity which is a destroying force in the thunderbolt carries our messages and warms our houses when diverted to safe uses. National feeling has been running too high not only in Germany but to some extent in nearly every people. Its indulgence has been almost as dangerous to peace as was its repression by the ignorant and short-sighted diplomatists of former generations. Recent experience has taught us to understand the limitations as well as the value of the principle of Nationality. Better things may be hoped from it in the future as it becomes more and more restrained and purified by the higher sentiment of an allegiance to mankind.

CHAPTER VIII

CONCERNING A PEACE LEAGUE

THE idea that action should be taken after this war to secure an enduring peace in the future, an idea at first derided as Utopian and afterwards denounced as a form of " pacificism," has begun to find favour among the Allied nations in Europe, and now receives in Britain an assent almost as general and hearty as it had already won in America. Statesman after statesman has blessed it. Nearly all the organs of public opinion that are worth regarding commend it. Trade Unions and other organizations of workers have given it a specially warm welcome. Thus it is scarcely necessary to-day to submit arguments on its behalf.[1] It is enough to refer to the words spoken by the leading statesmen of Britain and France, to the powerful advocacy of President Wilson, ex-President Taft, and Mr. Elihu Root in the United States, expressing, it cannot be doubted, the general sentiment of the American people, and especially to the despatch of January 8, 1917, in which the Allied Powers gave it their collective sanction. Nevertheless, in Great Britain at least, the idea still remains (to all but a few students) a vague conception, an aspiration that has taken no definite and tangible form. It is easy to talk of a Peace League. But

[1] It is hardly necessary to say that the Peace League discussed in the following pages is a totally different thing from the present Alliance of the " Entente Powers " formed to prosecute this war to a successful conclusion, and would be established after, and if possible immediately after, that conclusion, in order to make secure and permanent the peace then attained. All that I have to say relates to what may be done after the war has ended, though it is important to begin at once to consider the proper steps to be then taken.

in what definite way and for what specific purposes
are nations to combine? Who are the combining
nations to be? Will any combination stand firm and
endure? in power, in wisdom, in a sense of responsibility and in honesty of purpose? What machinery
can be created equal to a task so great as that of keeping the world's peace? The proposal is one of immense scope, and opens up all sorts of questions which
it would take a large book to explore and discuss. Into
the details of these questions I shall not venture. But
it may be profitable to state exactly what the essence
of the problem is, what sort of action it implies, what
obstacles confront those who try to solve it. The evil
to be dealt with is as old as mankind. Tribes were
already fighting in the Stone Age, as the remains of
their weapons show. The philosophers of the ancient
world assumed war to be the natural relation between
States. While the conditions of human society generally have been improving in other directions, in this
one direction they have grown worse. Man, as he
developed skill, soon found means of defending himself
against the wild beasts that used to terrify him. Still
advancing, he studied and subjugated the forces of
nature. He has learnt how to prolong his life and
how to cure most of his diseases. But while other
evils were being extinguished or mitigated, the evils
of war have increased. The present world conflict
is more terrible in the volume of slaughter and in the
physical and moral suffering it has brought on combatants and non-combatants than any which history
records.

Many remedies have been from time to time propounded, but only once has a serious attempt been made
to apply any. Christ taught that men should love one

another, even their enemies, and when the rulers of the world embraced Christianity it was expected that peace would overspread the world.   Athanasius, writing in the days of Constantine, declared that wars would end because Christians could not possibly fight one another. Centuries after his time sanguine spirits hoped that the Pope, as the spiritual, or the Emperor, as the temporal head of Christendom,[1] would bring the strife of Christian States to an end.   But Popes as well as Emperors were found who fomented war, or, like Julius II., themselves engaged in it.[2]

Now, when at last many peoples are again addressing their thoughts to find means of securing an enduring peace, two methods are proposed.   One, which is really the Christian method in a new dress, is to induce men to restrain their national patriotism, or national selfishness so far as to recognize, over and above their duty to their own State, an allegiance to Humanity at large.   They are to respect the rights of others equally with their own, and to cultivate what has been called an International or a Supernational Mind.   This remedy, if it succeeded, would be a complete remedy. But the spirit it enjoins has made little, if any, progress in recent years, and the most ardent optimists admit that no one can, as yet, foresee a time when it will prevail over the world.

Another method would be that of the Anarchists, who propose to destroy war by destroying the State as the power which makes war, or that which finds expression in the doctrine of the Bolshevists that if those whom they call " Capitalists " and " bourgeois " were extinguished and all men became " proletarians,"

---

1 See in particular Dante's treatise *De Monarchia.*
2 See the book of Erasmus, written two centuries after Dante, called *The Complaint of Peace.*   He refers to the case of Pope Julius, his contemporary.

national distinctions would be effaced and the causes
of war be therewith removed. These fantastic visions
need not delay us.

The only method with a promise of practical utility
that has been proposed for securing international peace
is that suggested by a consideration of the steps whereby
law and order have been established within every
civilized community. In primitive societies, and down
even to the Middle Ages, private wars were common.
Whoever had the power did that which was right in
his own eyes, making good his claims or redressing
his injuries by the strong hand. After a time the evils
of violence being felt, custom established rules for
settling disputes. An authority which was, or professed to be, impartial grew up, which adjudicated
according to these rules, and the collective power of
the community was called in to enforce the decisions
given by the judicial authority. By these means law
and order were established within each State. No
such means have been applied to the settlement of
disputes between States, because rules recognized by
States as binding them have not existed, because there
has not been an impartial authority to determine disputes arising between them, because even in cases where
nations have agreed to set up such an authority on
a particular occasion there has been no power strong
enough to enforce obedience to its decisions. If these
three things could be created, viz.: (1) A body of
rules constituting a law governing the relations of
States, (2) impartial tribunals to decide controversies
between States according to that law, and (3) a supra-
national power to compel obedience to the judgments
of those tribunals, there would be a security against
violence done by one nation to another resembling

that which now exists within each State against violence done by one citizen to another.

How, then, can these three requisites for international peace be created?

The first requisite is a law which independent States will recognize as binding. The rules which now go by the name of international law are, as everybody knows, not really laws in the strict sense of the word. Many of them have the authority of justice and good sense behind them. Many have the authority of a custom long settled and observed. Others, again, though not rules of universal application, have been embodied in treaties between two or more States, and are therefore binding in honour on those States. But none of these principles or customs or obligations of honour created by contract can be relied on as certain to be obeyed. No principle of right is based on a more solid foundation of justice than that the territory of a peaceful neutral must not be violated by a belligerent power. But this did not prevent the German Government from invading and ruining Belgium. A solemn promise was made by the Great Powers to one another at the Hague in 1907 to abstain from the use of poisonous gases in war. This did not prevent the German Government from resorting to that cruel method. To the means of making so-called international law effective by providing for its enforcement we must presently return. Meantime we have to ask who is to draft and enact the rules which are to bind States or nations in the future. Evidently this must be done by States themselves. They must select competent men to prepare the rules, and must after discussion enact them, each State pledging itself to the others to a full and loyal obedience of what they have conjointly declared to be the law that shall thereafter govern their relations to one another. Any State that refuses to join will, of course, not be technically bound by the law enacted; but that law will, nevertheless, have a much higher authority than international rules have hitherto possessed, for it will embody the mind and will of at least a considerable number of States who will be concerned to apply, extend and defend it.[1]

How is this body of international law, once created, to be applied to the controversies that may arise between States? Disputes must, of course, be expected to arise between nations as they do between individuals within a State. Some way must be found of settling them by peaceful methods, since the nations have agreed to forgo war.

This method will obviously be the establishment of a Tribunal, which can inspire respect by the learning and experience, the skill and the impartiality of the judges who compose it. Such an international tribunal will resemble the Courts of Arbitration set up in time past for a special purpose by two litigant States, such as that which, in 1910, consisting of eminent jurists selected from the panel of the Hague Court, happily settled the question of 120 years' standing between Great Britain and the United States over the Newfoundland fisheries. Treaties now exist between Great Britain and the United States, as also between France and other Powers and the United States, providing for arbitration by Courts so specially set up for such occasions. What is now proposed is a Permanent Tribunal which shall not need a special treaty made for each occasion, but one to which any State shall be entitled to appeal for justice against another, that other

1 It has been suggested that every law enacted should require the consent of at least two-thirds of the members of the League.

being bound to recognize the jurisdiction and put in an appearance. Arrangements would of course be made that those judges of the tribunal who were to hear the particular case should not be drawn from either of the contestant States.

Controversies of a legal character easily admit the use of this judicial procedure. Where a dispute turns upon facts, or upon the interpretation of a contract (*i.e.* a treaty) between the litigant States, the issue is one which a Court of Arbitration can determine. But many of the differences or suspicions or grounds of ill-will that induce war between States have not this legal or justiciable character.[1] Whoever will examine the circumstances that brought about most of the disputes that ended in war during the last seventy years will find that very few are such as a judicial tribunal could have dealt with by legal methods. Where the question is one of what is called National Honour, and is perhaps mere national vanity, where the difficulty lies in sentiment or in views of material interests involved, where one nation does not trust the other, or nurses a sullen resentment for past injuries, these methods avail little. What is wanted is something less rigid and more elastic, not Adjudication but Conciliation. In some of the disputes just referred to as having caused recent wars, the mediation of even one impartial State might have had a fair chance of success, and that of a group of impartial States a better chance.

1 This is true of the wars of 1853 (Great Britain and France against Russia), of 1866 (Prussia and Austria), of 1870 (Germany and France), of 1877 (Russia and Turkey), of 1898 (U.S.A. and Spain), of 1899 (Great Britain and the Transvaal), of 1904 (Russia and Japan), of 1909 (Italy and Turkey), of 1912 (Balkan States and Turkey), of 1913 (Serbia, Bulgaria, and Greece).

Disputes are said to be " justiciable " when they relate to the interpretation of a treaty or turn on any question of international law, or on the existence of any fact which would, if established, constitute a breach of any international obligation. or as to the nature and extent of the reparation to be made for any such breach. When it is doubtful whether a question is or is not " justiciable," the point might be referred to the Tribunal for decision.

In most of them, moreover, a careful investigation of the sources of friction and of the complaints which each disputant had against the other would have enlightened the world at large as to the merits of the controversy. And if during the period occupied by such an investigation — a period of, say, four or six months — each disputant had been required to refrain from military operations, the mere lapse of time would have allowed passions to cool and would have enabled the public opinion of the world to express itself. Even in 1914 it is possible that if each State had been compelled, on pain of incurring the hostility of nations not directly concerned, to refrain from setting its armies in motion for a period of six months, war would have been averted.

There is therefore an evident need for the creation by the combined peace-loving and peace-ensuing nations of an organ suited to cases which are incapable of legal determination. This organ would be most useful if it were permanent, taking the form of a Council composed of persons representing each of the combining States, persons possessed not necessarily of legal attainments, though these would always be valuable, but of historical, geographical, diplomatic, and political knowledge, and, above all, of tact and experience in public affairs.

The function of such a Council would be to examine and consider controversies between States which were endangering their friendly relations, and to endeavour to find means for pacifically adjusting differences, by removing their causes or by propounding a reasonable compromise between conflicting claims. This would be attempted by diplomatic methods, but in some cases, especially where the States concerned seemed unamenable to persuasion, it would be useful to publish a report upon the situation, setting out the case made by each State, delivering the opinion of the Council upon the merits of the issues, and recommending an adjustment calculated to reduce tension and avert hostilities.   Such a Report would have a double value.   It might affect the minds and allay the passions of the contending parties, for it usually happens that each nation is fed up, by its own politicians and its own press, with exaggerated and fallacious views of its own claims, views which moderate men are denounced as unpatriotic for seeking to correct.   At least one recent war could be mentioned which would never have come about had the people who were thus beguiled into it known the full truth.   Not less important would be the service a Report might render in providing other nations with the means of forming a just judgment on the respective claims of the disputant States.   Any war arising anywhere over the earth has now become an evil to the world which the public opinion of the world ought to be invoked to avert.   That opinion is a growing power.   Think of the efforts made from 1914 onwards by Germany on the one hand and the Entente Allies on the other to win it over to their side.   If its weight were thrown in favour of either party it might deter the other from resorting to hostilities.

It seems better not to bestow on a Council of Conciliation any executive powers.   It may work more freely without them.   But for the purposes of enquiry and report it must be allowed time.   Months might be required from the moment when the danger of war appeared before the suggestions of the Council could be addressed to the parties involved and a fair chance secured for mediation.   Here, however, a grave difficulty presents itself.   Time has become more important than ever in war.   The promptitude with which the

German armies flung themselves across the Bohemian frontier in 1866 and the French frontier in 1870 gave to them, as to the Japanese armies in 1903, an initial advantage which affected the whole course of the campaign.   An ambitious nation that has made up its mind to fight will not likely forgo such an advantage.   It will desire to strike at once and strike hard, as Germany struck in 1914.   How is it to be induced to hold its hand till the voice of reason can be heard, till methods of Conciliation have had their chance?   Only by the interposition of a power superior to its own.

This consideration brings us sharply back to the question of Compulsion.   We have seen that it is idle to construct a system of international law without Force behind it.   Force and nothing but Force will restrain those to whom Might is Right.   A tribunal will be ineffective without some means of giving effect to its decisions.   A body selected to apply methods of conciliation will be little regarded unless it represents potential power, ready to be put in action by those who have created it.   And it is even more plain that States disposed to reject arbitration or conciliation will fall upon their neighbours as suddenly as they can unless the fear of a Force stronger than their own deters them.

The Force needed for all these purposes must be greater than any one violent and rapacious State or any probable combination of rapacious States can put forth. It is to be found in a League for securing Peace, able to make its Will to Peace prevail against the Will to Violence of bellicose nations.   This is the sort of League which the men of good-will over the world now desire to establish.

Among the other questions that arise as to how such a League can be created and what is the machinery by which it must work, I will deal with two before proceeding to consider the obstacles that must be surmounted before the League can be created. One is: Who shall be the members of the League? There has been much discussion as to what States shall be admitted. It is asked: " Why not make it a World League and invite all States to join? " It is answered: " There may well be States which would enter with no honest purpose, but rather to conceal their own selfish aims, or possibly to try to wreck the enterprise. To admit such would be dangerous." Are we then to admit none but free nations (*i.e.* democracies), because such nations only can be trusted to desire justice and peace? This would furnish a line of discrimination nearly yet not quite complete, because there might well be a truly constitutional monarchy or republic, whose government, although not wholly popular, might be trusted to become an honest and useful member of a Peace League. Chile, a constitutional republic but hardly to be called a democracy, is an instance. It must also be observed that there are in the Western hemisphere some so-called " republics " which are really military tyrannies, and so not fit to be received. Their rulers, having no responsibility either to their subjects or to the public opinion of the world, could not be trusted. Perhaps, therefore, the simplest plan may be to leave it to those States which first form the League to decide whom they will admit as partners. It will be the interest of these original members to strengthen the combination by including in it all States whose loyalty to its principles is beyond question.

It has been often asked whether Germany and Austria can be admitted. Is not this a question that cannot be answered till the end of the war has come? Should that much-desired moment see a repentant

Germany, "regenerate in the spirit of its mind," its claim to co-operate could not be denied and would indeed be welcomed.   We do not desire a League against Germany, but one in which a new, de-Prussianized Germany would honestly join in promoting a World Peace.   But should the present military oligarchy be still in the saddle, ferocious and unscrupulous, dominating a too submissive people, he would be a sanguine man who could believe that such a Government as that of the Prussian Junkers has shown itself to be would join the League except with a purpose of undermining it.   Rather would its threatening presence require either the continuance of the existing Alliance of the Entente Powers or the maintenance by the future Peace League of military and naval armaments amply sufficient to hold it in check.

The other question is: What shall be the Organs of the League? Of these Organs two have been already mentioned, the Court of Arbitration and the Council of Conciliation, the former of which might consist of from twelve to fifteen judges, while the number of the latter, which would probably act largely by Committees, might run up to twenty, the members of each being chosen from the nations composing the League, and all the larger of these nations being represented on the Council.   Besides these bodies there will be needed another for the purpose, essential after the shocks which the war has given to the fabric of international law, of rebuilding that system of rules in a fuller, clearer, and more authoritative form.   For this there must be a sort of legislature, composed of representatives of all the States within the League, each appointing at least one member.   Rules drafted by this body, which might be called the Conference or Congress of the League, would be submitted to the Governments of the Component States, to be by them either adopted or referred back for further consideration till finally approved. If adopted by a prescribed majority of the States, they would become binding on all the States, and constitute, subject of course to subsequent amendments from time to time, a Code of International Law.

A second Organ also may be found necessary in order to make effective the machinery described for preventing war. A Court of Arbitration and a Council of Conciliation will lose half their value if there be not some means of compelling disputant States within the League, and also any State outside it which had a controversy with a State within it, to resort to one or other of these methods before taking hostile action. There must be executive action in the background, and means for determining when and how to act must be provided. Two such means may be suggested. One is for the Governments of the States within the League, at the request of any one of their number, to consider forthwith together what action they will jointly take. The other is to constitute a permanent Executive of the League, consisting of representatives chosen by the States, which would meet in conclave as soon as signs of danger appeared and recommend the measures of coercion required. Arguments may be advanced in favour of either method.

Some of our friends in America who have given much thought to this subject conceive that the League ought to have two other Organs also. One of these would be a tribunal to decide, where the point seemed doubtful, whether any particular controversy between States ought to be referred to the Court of Arbitration or to the Council of Conciliation. They suggest that a body, which might be called the Court of Conflicts,

should be formed from the same members of the Arbitration Court and some members of the Council of
Conciliation to determine such cases.   The other
Organ would be a Court in which suits raising pecuniary
claims might be brought by individual citizens or cor-
porations of one country against the Government of
some other country.   Cases of this kind are frequent,
and often involve protracted diplomatic discussions
and long delays.   It would be convenient to make regular provision for them.   The judges to hear and decide them might be a branch of the Court of Arbitration.[1]

It has been asked whether every State is to be equally
represented in the various Organs of the League.   As
respects the Arbitral Tribunal and the Council of Conciliation, since the excellence of these bodies depends
on the personal qualities of their members, the best men
ought to be selected, wherever they can be found, but
the large majority of such men will obviously be found
in the five or six greatest States.   In the Conference or
Congress, since the rules it prepares are meant to be
generally binding, every State must have a voice, though
the greater would be entitled to a larger representation
than such small States as those of South-Eastern Europe
and of the tropical parts of the New World.   Equality
between Powers like France and the United States on
one side and Montenegro or Salvador on the other
would be not justice but injustice.   Still more clearly
will the great States have larger representation in any
executive authority, since it is upon them that the duty
of enforcing the decisions of the League will chiefly
or perhaps wholly fall.

As respects the executive action of the League, *i.e.*

---

1 A Court of this kind was created in 1912 by a treaty between Great Britain
and the U. S. for the determination of claims, some of which were more than
a century old.

the prevention of a recourse to war before the Arbitral Tribunal has given its decision, or before the Council of Conciliation has accomplished its work of enquiry and mediation, two questions have to be answered. Ought the League to confine itself to securing either Arbitration, or a period of time sufficient for enquiry and for Conciliation, leaving the disputant parties alone so soon as one or other method has been applied? Or ought it to go further and compel, by coercive means, those disputant parties to obey the decision of the Tribunal given in a justiciable controversy, or to comply with the recommendations of the Council in other (*i.e.* non-justiciable) matters? The American League to Enforce Peace have inclined to the former plan, thinking that it is unwise to attempt, at present, anything more far-reaching. Others conceive that this is not enough, because a powerful and aggressive State might disregard the decision given or recommendation made and proceed to attack its weaker opponent. Nothing, they say, can be relied on to prevent this and give due protection to the weak except the knowledge that the whole force of the League will be arrayed against aggression.

Whichever view may be taken as to this point, there will be two engines of compulsion available. One is the application of armed force. The League must have at its disposal military and naval resources sufficient to protect any of its members who accept the decision, or (as the case may be) recommendations against an antagonist who disregards them. This raises the question whether the League should maintain a regular standing army and navy under the control of its Executive, or be content to call upon the several States that compose it to make up such an army by contributing their prescribed contingents. The former plan would make military operations more effective, for unity of command could be better secured, but the latter, as leaving greater independence to the several Powers, would probably be preferred by their Governments.

Supposing this latter plan to be approved, it has been suggested that the States comprising the League might be divided into two classes: (1) The Great Powers, who would be bound to put their military and naval forces at the disposal of the Executive; and (2) the Minor Powers, which would assume belligerency against any State attacking a member of the League, but would not be required by the Executive to contribute military or naval support, though they would join in whatever measures of economic compulsion might be decreed.[1]

This compulsion would be the grand method applicable against a recalcitrant State. It might be applied as a first step, to be followed, if necessary, by military action. It would consist in a commercial, financial, and possibly also a postal and telegraphic boycott. All the members of the League may refuse to send goods to it or receive goods from the offending State, and may forbid their citizens to lend money to it. It may be cut off from communications by post or telegraph. All supplies to it of raw materials needed for industries may be stopped and all banking transactions interdicted. Objection to such measures of commercial restriction has been taken on the ground that they might operate unequally among the members of the

---

1 Those who had talked of boycotting Germany and Austria as soon as this war is over had much better wait to see how the war ends. How can they declare that the war ought to be prosecuted till the German Government has been made powerless for evil, and also assume that the Government will, at the end of the war, be as powerful for evil as ever, able to resume its insidious schemes against the industries and resources of other countries? If it is then still able to do so, by all means let us deal vigorously with such a menace. Most of us, however, believe that if, even after realizing to the full the disaster to which the perfidy of her rulers has led, Germany still remains unrepentant, she can be disabled from all such plots.

League itself, affecting the industry and commerce of some members much more than those of others. This might conceivably happen, but after all such countries would suffer more by war.

The refusal to a manufacturing country of raw materials for its industries and a market for its products would be a penalty it would scarcely venture to defy. Such a method might often be speedier than war, and quite as effective. But its efficacy would depend upon its being reserved as a weapon to check some aggressive action against a member of the League. An economic boycott applied in normal peace times by one nation or group of nations against the legitimate trade of a foreign country would be a means of provoking rather than of preventing war, and might not be resorted to by the Allied nations against Germany and Austria, as some have suggested should be done *in any event* after the war. As Mr. Lloyd George has well said: " We must not arm Germany with a real wrong." A League honestly desiring peace could not take such action except as a penal measure against an aggressive State hereafter threatening its neighbours with hostilities.

Other useful objects which might fall within the scope of the League's activities have been put forward. One is the protection of native races in tropical countries from exploitation by European Governments or European adventurers.[1] Another is the elaboration of rules for securing the free passage of goods by rivers or railroads from inland countries to the sea. A third is the making of regulations which would reduce the spread of disease (and especially of epidemics) from one country to another. A fourth is the rendering of guidance, as, for instance, by providing capable officials, to back-

1 An interesting suggestion as to such action in Africa has been made by Sir S. Oliver, formerly Governor of Jamaica.

ward countries that need them, or by advice as to their financial engagements. A fifth is the consideration of measures for improving industrial conditions on parallel lines in different countries. Every region, every people, is now more closely bound to every other than in former days, and each has become more dependent on the others for weal or woe, so that without pursuing the illusion of a " world government " there are many ways in which the joint action of nations may enure to the benefit of all.

These schemes, however, I must pass by — they are too complicated for brief treatment — to speak of one more nearly related to that preservation of peace which will be the main aim of the League. It is the question of Armaments. The gigantic armies and navies — to which we must now add the increasing air forces — which great nations have been maintaining, have proved to be not so much, as was often represented, an insurance against war as rather an incitement and temptation to it. They have imposed a crushing burden upon the peoples of the Great Powers, a burden which must become greater as science goes on producing new and ever costlier warlike engines and devices. Must it not be a main function of any Peace League to bring armies and navies and air fleets down to a modest level and keep them from hereafter expanding?

Few will deny that this is an admirable aim, entirely within the scope of the League. Nothing would be more helpful. It is indeed essential. But how is it to be carried out, even if the manufacture of armaments be kept entirely within the hands of Governments? Doubters ask: " Upon what principles can the proportions of armed forces be allotted to different nations be determined? What security can each have that others will not exceed the limit prescribed? What means can be found for detecting and checking the prohibited increase of their forces and their stores of munitions? Estimates presented to a Legislature purporting to be for one purpose may be covertly transferred to another purpose. The German Reichstag is said to have been in this way often overreached. Many kinds of war materials and contrivances may be secretly manufactured. Articles needed for peace purposes may be capable of being rapidly adapted to the purposes of war. How are such things to be prevented?" These are questions which we must hope to see answered, but the answers are not yet forthcoming. Since it is evident that the peace-loving nations cannot reduce their respective armaments till they have a ground for security in an armed Force upon which they can rely to defend each one of them against attack from outside, this is a matter of urgent importance.

Other objections of wide scope which have been taken to the scheme of a Peace League deserve consideration. It is better to face them at the outset and see how they can be met than hasten forward in a spirit of easy optimism.

1. It is argued that when a State enters into a permanent compact, binding itself to submit to Arbitration or Conciliation all its controversies with other States, it necessarily renounces some of its self-determination and sovereignty. Doubtless it does. But it does this whenever it concludes a treaty. Every contract a man makes creates an obligation limiting his antecedent freedom of action. But men make contracts because they expect to gain more in other ways than they lose in the particular part of their freedom they part with.[1] So does a State. Here the gain is immense. There will

---

[1] "The question for every contracting party in all forms of contract," says Sir F. Pollock, "is whether the portion of liberty he surrenders is adequately recompensed by the portion of reward or security he acquires."

doubtless be cases in which a State will dislike a summons to defend its conduct before a Court of Arbitration or a Council of Conciliation. But this must be faced if the League is to attain its ends; and we may expect from such a Court and Council as the League will create an upright and impartial handling of the matters referred to them. Even the strongest State has more benefits to expect for itself from the security of a world peace than it could obtain by war, while the benefit to humanity at large is immeasurable.

2. I need not stop to refute the Prussian doctrine that frequent wars are needed to maintain the virility and courage of a nation,—" a drastic medicine for the human race," says Treitschke, " which God will always provide,"— for that doctrine has found its completest disproof in the present war. The two great nations of the world who have least desired war, thought of war, prepared themselves for war, have been the peoples of Britain and America. They ought, on the Prussian theory, to have been found when war came feeble, spiritless, effeminate. But what have we seen? Britain raised in three years an army of five millions, most of them volunteers, and these men have come from the pursuits of peace, the rich as gladly as the poor, to show a valour and an endurance never surpassed by their ancestors in the fighting days of the Middle Ages. The men of America, even (if that be possible) more pacific in their spirit, have flown to arms and thrown themselves into the conflict with a whole-hearted enthusiasm which has amazed those who did not know what the American people are. Heroism is not made by military drill and practice. It dwells in the hearts and the ideals of a people, and while these are sound, it responds to the call of duty.

But a word must be given to another argument. It

is sometimes said that the patriotic sentiment will be weakened by a League which relies upon and seeks to foster the sentiment of human brotherhood, making men recognise an allegiance to mankind, a sense of what he owes to its common welfare. But is this so? Will this effect follow? Is there not room for both feelings? Why should a citizen feel his duty to his country any the less because he feels a duty to his larger fatherland the world? Does a man cease to be a patriotic Virginian or Californian because he recognises a higher allegiance to the United States? Has Scottish national pride proved incompatible with zeal to serve the United Kingdom and the British Commonwealth of Nations? Is a father less likely to love his family and do his best for them because he is a public-spirited citizen, always at the service of his neighbours and his city, or a less earnest and devoted member of his own Church because he wishes to see all the Churches brought together in a reunited Christendom? Love, and the expression of Love in duty gladly done, are things of which it can be said that the more we give the more we have to give, according to the famous lines:

> I could not love thee, Dear, so much,
> Loved I not honour more.

3. To extend to every State a guarantee against an attack by any other State might (it is argued) have the effect of perpetuating injustices or grievances suffered by a part of the population of a State, for some other State might be thus prevented from compelling, by threats of war, the redress of those grievances. The existing conditions would be stereotyped, however unfair they might be to some sections of a State's sub-

jects, however likely to go on breeding discontent.[1] Suppose the Government of a country to treat part of its subjects as Austria has treated the Czechs, or Prussia the Poles of Posen, or as the Spanish Government treated Cuba before 1898. Is a Peace League to arrest all efforts from without, made by a nation sympathizing with these subjects, to remove the grievances they suffer from? It may be answered that under the scheme outlined above such grievances could be brought before, and be dealt with by, the Council of Conciliation. But the Council would not have the power to extinguish them should its recommendations be rejected. May there not then be a case either for allowing interference by a sympathetic State or for empowering the League to interfere? If the matter transcends the functions of the Council of Conciliation, the members of the League might (it has been suggested) meet in Congress to consider it.

4. Does there exist a due supply in the world of the persons fit for such difficult duties as those which the scheme entrusts to the Tribunal of Arbitration and for the still more delicate functions of the Council of Conciliation? Judges of sufficient legal learning and skill as are required may perhaps be found to staff the Tribunal, though there are none too many. But the men qualified for the Council are extremely few. A knowledge of history and geography, of diplomacy, and of the political conditions of the different countries of the world is needed, for the work is international. And besides the tact and good sense required, the Councillors must have that superiority to national prejudices and that reputation outside their own country which

---

1 This difficulty points to the propriety of endeavouring to remove (so far as possible) at the end of the present war all such sources of future trouble.

would give them a truly international authority. As to this it may be answered that under the new conditions we hope for, the supply of men required will tend to increase, and each people will know more of those who reach eminence and inspire confidence in other countries.

5. Can any League of Nations be trusted to withstand the temptations which will assail its members? Timidity, jealousy, self-interest will not cease to affect Governments. Intrigues proceeding from the ill-will of States outside the League, or from some treacherous Government of one of the States inside it, must be contemplated as possible, intrigues designed to bring about a failure to perform the obligation to join in applying compulsion. To use a colloquial phrase, "Will the nations in the League play up?" If even one nation fails at the critical moment, others may make that failure a pretext for withdrawal. Then the League would fall to pieces, and those who, in reliance on it, had reduced their armaments would be exposed to sudden danger. Some one may say, "These are prophecies, and, according to the proverb, you cannot argue with a prophet, but you can disbelieve him." Here, however, there is no case for confident disbelief. The risks predicted cannot be lightly dismissed. Have we not just seen men who came into power by a revolution in a great empire repudiate the solemn engagements which its Government had made three years before, and not only abandon the Allies whom it had itself drawn into a tremendous conflict, but deliver over to their enemy regions of immense strategic importance, which were immediately occupied and used by that enemy against them? There are, however, risks which must be faced where the greatness of the aim in view makes it worth while to go on. In this instance we

may weigh some considerations which inspire hope. Should a League to Enforce Peace be now formed, and should it come before long to include all, or nearly all, the great free and peace-loving Powers, its members will have time to form a habit of joint action and mutual confidence before any severe strain is put upon the obligations they have undertaken. The exhaustion and impoverishment caused by the present war will prevent any Power, however aggressive its spirit, from being able to threaten its neighbours for a good many years to come. Within those years the League may become an established institution, liable no doubt to find matter for controversy in the changing relations of countries to one another, but not likely to push its controversies to extremes. International relations may be raised to a higher plane of honour and justice. Threats of war may go out of fashion among those who remember what the sufferings of war were. Thus the sense of duty to mankind at large and to the great common aim of peace will have time to ripen and become durable in the minds of the next generation as the public opinion of the world, which is on the whole pacific, and ought to grow more than ever pacific while it remembers what misery this war has brought upon this generation, acquires more and more influence on every nation. The mere fact that the League exists as an organization created to represent the joint interest of all men of good will cannot but help to nourish and develop the spirit of goodwill and human brotherhood.

Let us remember that the wars of the past have been mostly made by despots, or by oligarchies; and it is by them that the faith of treaties has been mostly broken. But now, in nearly all the great States, power has passed to the people, but the people can be trusted better than the monarchs or the oligarchs of former days, both to realize the value of peace and to do all they can to secure it. Democracies also have been sometimes swept by passion or lured into war by misrepresentation; yet they are likely to feel a clearer duty both to refrain from aggression and to check it when attempted by others. They will better recognize the obligations of international honour and good faith, and their responsibility to mankind at large. They will feel more respect for the public opinion of the world.

Once the League of Peace has been established, its very existence will embody in visible form the principle of the solidarity of free nations, and will foster the sentiment of human brotherhood. Every year that it lives on ought to increase its moral authority and strengthen the respect for the decisions of its Courts.

These are hopes, not certainties. But they are not dreams, there are solid grounds for the hopes; and this time is one in which we must hope, for if we do not hope we must despair. If we do not try to end war, war will end us. Moments come when evils have grown so frightful that new and bold experiments must be tried to escape from them; times when men must go forward in the strength of faith and hope.

It is among the masses of the people in this country that the warmest zeal has been shown for this beneficent idea. It is from the great democracy of the West and its leaders, President Wilson and others, that the most powerful impulse has come. The difficulties are doubtless great. Much wisdom, much skill, will be needed to surmount them. But the people must supply the motive power. They must push statesmen forward. They must join in guiding the policy of the League and to help it by their watchful sympathy. And behind the sympathy there must be to inspire it the sense of a great and high motive. Our motives and those of our Allies in this war are purer than ever were seen in a war before. We are fighting for Righteousness against Wickedness, fighting to protect the weak, to secure the recognition of conscience and duty as the highest powers, the powers on whose rule the safety of the world depends. It is this motive that has brought America to our aid, America, which had no interest of her own to secure, and had hitherto watched from afar, in happy security, the strifes and sorrows of the Old World.

It may be convenient to sum up in a few propositions the reasons for creating a Peace League and the essential features which it ought to possess.

1. The prevention of future wars will be, after this war has ended, one of the supreme needs of the world.

2. War can be prevented only by submitting for it methods of Arbitration and Conciliation as the means of settling international disputes.

3. Arbitration and Conciliation cannot succeed unless there is Compulsive Force behind them.

4. Compulsive Force can be secured only by the co-operation and combination of peace-loving nations, *i.e.* by a League to Enforce Peace.

5. Every member of such a League must undertake to accept Arbitration or Conciliation in any controversy it may have with another member.

6. The League shall undertake to defend any one of its members who may be attacked by any other State which has refused to accept Arbitration or Conciliation.

7. The League will require four organs for its action: (*a*) a Tribunal to arbitrate on justiciable controversies, (*b*) a Council of Conciliation to enquire into and apply mediation in non-justiciable controversies, (*c*) a representative Conference or Congress to amend,

develop, and codify international law, and (*d*) an Executive Authority to decide on the time and methods of applying (and to supervise the application of) measures for compelling disputant States to submit to arbitration and to allow time for Conciliation before resorting to hostilities.

8. The methods of Enforcement may be either the use of economic pressure or the use of armed force, or both, as the Executive Authority may determine.

9. The League shall adopt any measures it finds to be practicable for bringing about a general reduction of military and naval armaments.

These may be taken as the chief points on which most of those who have been advocating the project in Britain and America are agreed. Other points of importance, but on which some difference of opinion exists, are the following:

(*a*) What shall be the principle regulating the admission of States to a Peace League?

(*b*) Shall all the members of the League (great and small) have equal powers and responsibilities, or, if not, how shall these be distributed?

(*c*) How shall the persons to serve on the Tribunal of Arbitration and on the Council of Conciliation be chosen?

(*d*) Shall the Executive Authority of the League consist of persons representing the Governments of the States who are its members, or how otherwise?

(*e*) Shall the Council of Conciliation have power to act when it sees dangers which threaten peace looming up, without being invoked by a disputant State?

(*f*) Shall the League have a standing army and navy, or shall it obtain its necessary forces by summoning the contingents of the States (or of the greater States) when the need for military action arises?